ROUTLEDGE LIBRARY EDITIONS:
WORK & SOCIETY

Volume 6

EMPLOYMENT AND INCOME DISTRIBUTION IN THE AFRICAN ECONOMY

EMPLOYMENT AND INCOME DISTRIBUTION IN THE AFRICAN ECONOMY

JAMES FRY

Routledge
Taylor & Francis Group
LONDON AND NEW YORK

First published in 1979 by Croom Helm Ltd.

This edition first published in 2024
by Routledge
4 Park Square, Milton Park, Abingdon, Oxon OX14 4RN

and by Routledge
605 Third Avenue, New York, NY 10158

Routledge is an imprint of the Taylor & Francis Group, an informa business

British Library Cataloguing in Publication Data
A catalogue record for this book is available from the British Library

ISBN: 978-1-032-80236-7 (Set)
ISBN: 978-1-032-81266-3 (Volume 6) (hbk)
ISBN: 978-1-032-81271-7 (Volume 6) (pbk)
ISBN: 978-1-003-49896-4 (Volume 6) (ebk)

DOI: 10.4324/9781003498964

Publisher's Note
The publisher has gone to great lengths to ensure the quality of this reprint but points out that some imperfections in the original copies may be apparent.

Disclaimer
The publisher has made every effort to trace copyright holders and would welcome correspondence from those they have been unable to trace.

EMPLOYMENT AND INCOME DISTRIBUTION IN THE AFRICAN ECONOMY

JAMES FRY

CROOM HELM LONDON

Croom Helm Ltd, 2-10 St John's Road, London SW11

British Library Cataloguing in Publication Data

Fry, James
Employment and income distribution in the African economy.
1. Income distribution – Zambia 2. Income distribution – Africa 3. Labor supply – Zambia
4. Labor supply – Africa
I. Title
339.2'09689'4 HC517.R42315

ISBN 0-85664-715-2

Printed in Great Britain by
Biddles Ltd, Guildford, Surrey

CONTENTS

INTRODUCTION

The subjects of the present volume, namely the growth of wage employment in a developing economy and the distribution of income within the same economy, are already familiar themes for research. Therefore, some justification is required for the presentation of the study that follows. The main one I would offer is that, while there is a substantial literature on each of the subjects considered here, there are all too few attempts to integrate them in any detail.

The Zambian economy is particularly suitable for an analysis of the relationship between economic growth and income distribution. Within 80 years, Zambia has followed an admirably well documented path from a position as one of the poorest, least developed African economies to its current status as the most highly urbanised independent African state. In the course of this progress, the economy has had to face structural problems that have, at some time or another, characterised the range of other economies in the same continent. Hence, a study of Zambia should throw light upon many aspects of the labour markets elsewhere in Africa.

During the 80-year period under review, Zambia has evolved from being a classic example of a colonial economy, in which primitive accumulation along Marxist lines occurred with stark simplicity, to become an independent state with a large export enclave heavily dependent upon foreign skills and capital. In between these two stages came the 35 years in which the export enclave developed in a strongly colonial environment.

The first four chapters of this book concentrate upon describing the impact of each of these three phases of development upon the labour force. In the course of the exposition, several particular points of interest stand out as worthy of note. During the first phase, for example, one notes the extreme reliance upon coercive measures, such as the imposition of heavy taxation accompanied by controls upon peasant agriculture and restrictions upon traditional non-agricultural activities, to force a substantial proportion of the labour force to offer itself for wage employment.

The emergence of a large source of demand for labour during the second phase of development coincided with a remarkable shift in employers' attitudes towards their employees. Instead of relying upon coercion, employers, notably those in the new copper mines, started to try to make wage employment attractive to workers. By doing so they hoped to reduce the exceptionally high rates of labour turnover that they were experiencing, and thereby maximise their return from the investment represented by the costs of training local labour. Skilled employment, however, remained the preserve of expatriates. This led to a very sharp divergence between the average earnings of local and expatriate workers. At the same time, there emerged marked sectoral differences in average earnings that have continued to the present day. The copper mines became the employers paying the best wages, while commercial agriculture, which continued to employ crude methods of labour coercion until the 1950s, paid the lowest wages.

Towards the end of the 1950s came the first easing of the restrictions upon Africans in skilled employment, and the commencement of the third and most recent of the phases that this volume identifies. In the labour market, the first years of the 1960s were dominated by the vexed question of the unification of expatriate and local pay scales. Some sectors, including the Civil Service, opted for a strictly unified, non-racial scale, in which the spread between lower and higher incomes was immense. Other sectors, such as the copper mines, moved towards a dual structure. Eventually, after considerable industrial unrest, there evolved a new pay structure in which expatriates' salaries were separated from those of their local counterparts by a special expatriate allowance. In the process, the gap between urban wages and traditional sector incomes became magnified. Paradoxically, the growth in the relative importance of the urban sector in the economy had the effect of making the nationwide distribution of income look more equal towards the end of this period, but there is no reason to believe that the distribution of income within either the urban or rural sectors did, in fact, become more equal.

This paradox provides the justification for the framework of analysis adopted in the second half of this book. Four differentials are identified as fundamental to the pattern of income distribution. These are the rural/urban differential, the local/expatriate differential, the skilled/unskilled differential and sectoral wage differentials.

In practice, the first two differentials give rise to the greatest problems, since the narrowing of one automatically implies the widening of the other. In terms of policy formulation, however, the latter pair of differentials are also troublesome. If the unskilled workers' minimum wage is set near the level of rural incomes, the skilled/unskilled differential becomes very considerable. Yet, if the unskilled wage is raised so as to reduce the degree of income inequality among wage earners, this serves merely to exacerbate rural/urban inequalities.

The differentials between wage scales in different sectors cause further difficulties for policymakers. It would appear from the Zambian evidence that such differentials are more than mere institutionally determined legacies from the past. It is not simply pressures from trade unions that explain sectoral differentials. Instead they are closely related to the technological structures of the various sectors, in particular as these affect the capital intensity of production and the return from expenditures upon training. Thus there is a degree of inevitability about the pattern of income distribution within the urban sector, as long as wage bargaining is allowed to proceed relatively unimpeded by government intervention.

These are depressing conclusions for all those who, like myself, believe the existing degree of income inequality in Zambia to be excessive. Nevertheless, there are, even within the present constraints under which policymakers feel obliged to work, measures related, for example, to the system of pricing agricultural products, or to the determination of the statutory minimum wage, or to the relationship between qualifications and salaries, which could improve the present situation in Africa. Accordingly, in Chapters 7 and 8, I present a comparative analysis of official attempts at prices and incomes policies in Eastern Africa, followed by some reflections upon the lesson to be learnt from them.

Throughout this book, I confine myself to the experience of Zambia and, to a lesser extent, Eastern Africa. In view of the complexity of the issues that are considered, the analysis would run the risk of becoming superficial if many other economies were added to the list of those studied in this volume. Moreover, relatively little is likely to be added to the broad lines of the arguments presented here. The four income differentials described above are found in all African countries, and the problems of achieving the correct balance between the magnitudes of the various differentials apply with great force to them all. Hence the analysis contained here should be understood to have a relevance far beyond the borders of Zambia.

1 THE DISTRIBUTION OF EMPLOYMENT AND INCOMES IN NORTHERN RHODESIA—THE PERIOD BEFORE THE SECOND WORLD WAR

The pattern of growth of incomes and employment in Northern Rhodesia, and the related development of the modern sector, can be understood only in the context of the full set of forces at work upon the economy. These include the external and internal political influences, and the social pressures, reflecting a variety of responses to taxation, migrant labour, wage employment and urbanisation, for example, as well as the forces which one might consider to be more 'purely' economic. There can be no doubt that these factors are closely interrelated. Thus the economist's notion of, say, a labour supply curve, relating wages to the amount of labour offering itself for wage employment, cannot be determined in isolation from political decisions regarding the level, and form, of taxation and labour recruitment, or controls on the access of potential wage workers to alternative sources of cash incomes. Similarly a labour supply curve will conceal under its standard statement '*ceteris paribus*' a whole host of assumptions about the social relationships within the traditional modes of production and how these will respond to external stimuli.

In the four chapters which follow, describing the distribution of employment and incomes in Northern Rhodesia and Zambia, the labour market is analysed mainly from the perspective of an economist. However, the reader is asked to bear in mind the very important fact that the aggregated or average figures that are mentioned in the text may conceal a wealth of information that is available from studies in the other social sciences. In as many places as possible, these studies will be acknowledged in the text, but the interested reader is referred to the impressive range of material published by the Rhodes-Livingstone Institute and its successors for the best picture of the political and social influences acting upon the population of the country during the period we are examining.

The British South Africa Company

The first decade of the British South Africa (BSA) Company's presence in Northern Rhodesia had a limited impact upon the labour force of the country. In 1898, the company received only £2,300 and in 1899 only £3,800 in revenue from its administration in Northern Rhodesia. The BSA Company needed to increase its revenues to cover the administrative costs it was incurring in Northern Rhodesia, but it also required unskilled labour for its mineral properties in Southern Rhodesia. These twin objectives were met through the imposition of poll and hut taxes and the encouragement of labour recruitment throughout Northern Rhodesia. As a result of such action, native tax receipts moved ahead steadily from £6,400 in 1902 to £26,000 in 1905, to £54,000 in 1908 and to £72,000 in 1914.

The payment of taxes in kind was prohibited in 1905, so that wage labour became virtually the sole means by which Africans could meet their tax obligations. Yet despite the more effective collection of taxes, the BSA Company continued to run up annual deficits on its Northern Rhodesian territories of £50,000. The mineral potential of the country was considered to be poor, and so the only profitable alternative for sources of revenue that remained to the company was the encouragement of European commercial farming. Accordingly, good agricultural land was alienated from African farmers near the railway line, as well as in the Fort Jameson (Chipata) and Abercorn (Mbala) areas.

In order to reduce the range of alternatives to wage labour available to Africans, the restrictions upon African agriculture were increased. Traditional agricultural systems were weakened. For example, the crop failure and famine in the northern half of the country in 1907 may be largely attributed to official efforts to control *chitemene* 'slash and burn' methods of cultivation. The Lozi *sishanjo* drainage system of agriculture deteriorated steadily following the 1906 abolition of the institution of serfdom.

Parallel to the erosion of traditional systems of cultivation, the marketing network for African produce and the rural road system were left deliberately undeveloped. Furthermore, the authorities had little compunction about using direct intervention to prevent African cultivators from entering cash agriculture, if the other restraints proved ineffective. When the Kaonde sought to export maize to Katanga in 1910, the Acting Administrator of North Western Rhodesia prevented the transaction, believing that, since the Kaonde were of fine physique, 'it would seem to be a better policy to encourage the energies of the Bakahondi in the direction of mining rather than agriculture.'[1]

Even outside the agricultural sector, obstacles existed to prevent Africans from trying to earn money without having to resort to wage labour. Hawking and small trading were put beyond the reach of all but a few Africans by setting the annual hawker's licence fee at £2 10s, ten times as large as the Native Tax in some of the poorer parts of the country.

In the earliest days of the Native Tax, there can be little doubt that wage employment afforded the only means of livelihood compatible with earning enough to supplement the resultant reduced level of domestic agricultural production with purchases of food to maintain a household's standard of living above the level of subsistence.

It is the interpretation of the factors behind the continued supply of wage labour at subsistence wages beyond the first few years of taxation which is open to controversy. Against Arrighi's view that 'real wages remained at a level which promoted capitalist accumulation not because of the forces of supply and demand, but because of politico-economic mechanisms that ensured the "desired" supply at the "desired wage rate"',[2] there is Barber's belief that traditional agriculture is characterised by the existence of 'periodic disguised unemployment',[3] a state of affairs whereby, over long periods of time during the year, labour can be withdrawn from traditional agriculture without materially reducing output. Barber contends that

> only a small proportion of the indigenous population has a genuine option between selling crops and selling labour as methods for achieving high real incomes . . . In these circumstances, the supply of indigenous labour available to wage employers would initially be perfectly elastic. Further, as long as the volume of absenteeism of adult male workers did not alter the family's agricultural output, there would be no tendency for the supply of labour to lose its elasticity . . . [However] as the money economy grows, its requirements for African labour may swell to the point where a further withdrawal of manpower from the indigenous economy cannot be accomplished without upsetting its traditional productive processes. If the assumption of the Native administrators about the proportion of the adult males required to maintain the integrity of the indigenous economy is correct, then a withdrawal of more than 50 percent of its ablebodied males would lead to a sharp reduction in the agricultural output of the indigenous family . . . At this point, the supply of labour would cease to be perfectly elastic. To attract additional indigenous workers, a rise in the real wage would be required.[4]

This is the situation that Barber names 'quasi-full employment'.

In some traditional systems of agriculture there is sound reason for Barber's belief in the existence of periodic disguised unemployment. In *chitemene* cultivation, for example, a man's work was typically concentrated into two periods – the lopping of branches at the middle of the year and the fencing of fields six months later – although, even in this case, there were duties, such as hunting or house building and repair, which had to be attended to at other times of the year. Yet there is the incontrovertible evidence that, in many parts of the country, by the mid-1910s manpower had been withdrawn from the indigenous economy to the point where it had 'upset its traditional productive processes'.[5]

Many of the poorer districts of Zambia reported over 50 per cent of their potential taxpayers working outside their home districts at this time,[6] and by most criteria it would appear that traditional agriculture had been disrupted. Yet the evidence concerning the wages paid to Northern Rhodesian miners working in Southern Rhodesia is that they provided very little, if anything, for discretionary expenditures after the workers' basic food requirements and tax dues had been met. Charles van Onselen[7] has documented the high death rate of African miners from purely nutritional diseases, such as scurvy, which resulted from the poor mine rations, compounded by the lack of money to pay for the extra food that the miners needed.

The first nutritional surveys in Northern Rhodesia in the late 1930s (when Barber contends that the traditional sector still suffered from periodic disguised unemployment) and 1940s make it abundantly clear that, given the levels of absence of adult males in earlier decades, and given the fact that the real disposable wages of African workers changed little between 1900 and 1940, the ability of the rural economy to produce sufficient food for its population must have been seriously impaired ever since migration flows assumed the rates attained during the First World War.

Audrey Richards's survey of Bemba families near Kasama in 1937, and Betty Preston Thompson's 1947 study of the diet of mainly Bemba-speaking people in Lusaka and Serenje (like Kasama, a *chitemene* area) are summarised in Table 1.1, page 16.[8] As J. Clyde Mitchell comments in his foreword to the latter study: 'People who are short of food, because their traditional mode of production has suffered through the absence of men, may look upon labour centres primarily as a source of food'.

All the criteria for Barber's 'quasi-full employment' appear to have been met long before real wages started to rise. Yet, through the combined impact of the agricultural marketing system, which made it very difficult to convert a high marginal physical product in traditional agriculture into cash, and the District Officer's discretion in the collection of the Native Tax, an elastic supply of wage labour was forthcoming far beyond the point at which the traditional system of agriculture had been disrupted. To paraphrase Arrighi, it was the politico-economic mechanisms of capitalist accumulation, rather than the interaction of supply and demand, which ensured the 'desired' supply at the 'desired' wage rate.

Table 1.1: Average Adult Daily Diets

Item of diet	Lusaka (1947)	Serenje (1947)	Kasama* (1937)	Requirement level (1947)
Calories	3,700	2,077	1,706	3,000
Protein (g)	116.5	62.5	50.0	65
Fat (g)	68.2	16.1	13.0	90
Carbohydrate (g)	66.7	420	327	430
Calcium (mg)	407	1,789	145	500-800
Iron (mg)	40.5	35.8	16.1	20
Vitamin A (IV)	8,856	4,697	–	5,000
Aneurin (mg)	1.58	1.84	NA	1.8
Riboflavin (mg)	1.45	0.77	–	1.8-2.3
Nicotinic acid (mg)	20.0	12.1	–	15
Ascorbic acid (mg)	79	23.1	–	30

*The Kasama figures varied throughout the year. In the hunger months before the first harvest, 286 calories daily intake per adult was recorded in one family. The highest daily calories intake per adult for any family at any time of year was 3,164 calories. Contrast these figures with the 1937 Government scale for its African employees of 4,313 calories per day, and the 1937 proposed new (reduced) Rhokana mine scale of 3,663 calories per day.

End of BSA Company Rule

The BSA Company was successful in mobilising a wage labour force, but this still proved incapable of generating sufficient revenues to finance the territory's administration. After the First World War, the company took its first tentative steps towards taxing the European population, though the tax schedule was hardly punitive – a couple with two children had to earn £1,200 per annum before becoming liable to income tax, and the maximum marginal tax rate was only 15 per cent. This made little difference to the basic financial position of the territory, and accordingly the company, in 1924, handed over the administration to the British Government, while retaining for itself large areas of land, which it hoped to sell later, and all mineral royalties.

At the time of the change of administration in 1924, the economy was still divided, as it had been for the previous 20 years, into a modern wage sector, in which Europeans received around 100 times the subsistence wages paid to Africans, and a traditional sector, producing a negligible marketable surplus of commodities other than fish or cattle and from which a large proportion of the adult male labour force had been withdrawn. Within seven years, signs of change had appeared.

In some small measure, the minor improvement that occurred in the living standards of African workers in the late 1920s could be attributed to a more enlightened social policy pursued by the British Government. Unlike the BSA Company administration, the new colonial government was prepared to devote funds to African education; and in 1930 came the famous Passfield memorandum, acknowledging the 'paramountcy of native interests' over those of settlers. Yet one must not overstate the liberality of a colonial administration which, in 1928, delimited 71 million acres of land for African reserves, while reserving 9 million acres of the best agricultural land for Europeans, and which consistently spent much more on schools and social services for Europeans than it did for Africans.

More important as factors behind the signs of improvement in African economic circumstances were, in agriculture, the adoption of the plough in areas of Southern and Central Provinces, permitting farmers to farm more extensively; and in the remainder of the economy, the labour policies pursued by the newly developed copper mines on the Copperbelt.

The full impact of the adoption of the plough was not observed until the mid-1930s. African farmers' sales of maize, having increased from only a few hundred tonnes in the early 1920s to stabilise at around 3,000-4,000 tonnes in the late 1920s and early 1930s, moved up strongly to 10,000 tonnes in 1935 and to over 20,000 tonnes in both 1936 and 1937. From 1935, African farmers' sales accounted for 40 per cent of Northern Rhodesia's total maize sales and European producers became worried that the local market would suffer from excess supply. Therefore they persuaded the government to introduce a system of controls on maize and cattle marketing, which, in years of low prices and excess supply, would place the main burden of lower producer prices on African farmers.

The copper mines of the Copperbelt were first developed in earnest in 1928, following the discovery of new methods for treating low-grade sulphide ores. From 9,100 in April 1928, employment on Northern Rhodesian mines had jumped to 31,940 by September 1930. Given the well-developed nature of the recruitment of wage labour in the country, the rapidly growing requirements for mineworkers on the Copperbelt were met, at first, by diverting to the Copperbelt recruits who would hitherto have gone mainly to Southern Rhodesia; but with the retrenchment on the mines after late 1930, in the wake of the world economic depression, the mining companies found that they could rely upon voluntary workers presenting themselves for employment at the mines rather than upon recruited labour. In October 1931, the use of recruited labour finally ceased.

A number of reasons have been adduced for the changed pattern of labour supply after 1930. Baldwin has mentioned that workers had come to accept the unusual conditions of work involved in mining.[9] Of at least equal importance was the fact that long periods of enforced involvement in wage employment had converted former 'discretionary' items of cash expenditure into 'needs', and that the traditional indigenous technology was either incapable of meeting these needs or was unfamiliar to workers who had spent long periods in migrant wage employment. Wage employment thus became the only means open to many Africans for providing their requirements.[10]

The mining companies in 1932 increased the work load expected of each miner, and at the same time reduced African wages by a quarter or more; yet the employers found it unnecessary to return to the former coercive methods to ensure an adequate labour supply. In the circumstances, with the copper mines generating much more government revenue than the Native Tax, and large numbers of migrant workers offering themselves for employment, the *raison d'être* of the Native Tax vanished. This was gradually recognised by the authorities, who, in 1935, allowed tax defaulters the option, for the first time, of paying their tax by means of labour on public works.[11] In 1938, the tax was allowed to be paid in kind to District Officers: the wheel had turned full circle to the pre-labour-shortage days before 1905.

Stabilisation

The most significant development in the labour market in the period after 1924 was none of the features mentioned above. The policy change which overshadows all others was the adoption by the mines of the policy of stabilisation.[12] The mining industries of Central Africa did not take long to learn that the efficiency of African workers could be increased substantially by improving the physical condition of the workers, by means of better food and living conditions, and by training Africans to take on semiskilled tasks. However, the employers also realised that the returns from their investments in better nutrition and training would be substantial only if healthy workers with skills could be encouraged to work for longer periods than the former six-month contract.

In Katanga, in 1927, the copper mining companies introduced three-year minimum contracts, and transported whole families, rather than just the male worker, to the mine. After the first three years of this form of stabilisation, Austin Robinson records that the volume of ore extracted per man-shift at a major Katangese mine had risen by over 50 per cent.[13] The comparable figures presented on the output per man in Northern Rhodesian mines following stabilisation show a much greater increase, but the statistics were so distorted by the effects of the rundown in employment during the Depression as to be useful only as an indicator of a trend. Another indication of the trend in labour policy may be gleaned from the rise from zero to one quarter in the African proportion of miners with a blasting certificate between 1928 and 1932. Table 1.2, referring to Roan Antelope Mine, brings out the negative correlation between labour turnover rates and the proportion of workers accompanied by their families in town.

Table 1.2: Labour Turnover at Roan Antelope Mine, 1927-35

Year	Average African work force	% of workers who were married and accompanied by their families	Monthly turnover rate (%)
1927	1,093	20	24.1
1928	2,005	20	22.3
1929	2,999	21	17.2
1930	3,961	22	16.7
1931	4,729	26.6	11.3
1932	2,317	37.3	10.4
1933	3,075	43.4	7.5
1934	4,621	50.0	7.4
1935	4,513	52.2	3.2

Source: F. Spearpoint, 'The African Native and the Rhodesian Copper Mines', Supplement to *Journal of the Royal African Society*, July (1937), p. 53.

At first sight, it may seem odd that employers wanting to make employment in the mines so attractive to Africans that they become willing to remain with an employer for long periods of time should have reduced money wages as they did in 1932. In part, this was possible because the Depression so reduced the demand for labour that employers could virtually dictate wage levels. Of greater practical importance was the fact that, while money wages were falling, the combined monetary and non-monetary real incomes of mineworkers were rising. The drop in monetary wages was more than compensated for by the increase in income given in kind, such as rations, uniforms and housing. To the employers, the payment of income in kind was attractive not only because the mines could use their monopsonistic buying power to acquire goods at favourable prices, but also because they could then be confident that high incomes would be reflected in sound nutritional and hygiene conditions for their employees.

Income Distribution in 1938

By 1938, the economy had recovered from the worst effects of the Depression. Employment in the mines had regained the high levels touched in 1930; while commercial agriculture, after the shocks of the mid-1930s, had reverted to a position where it could sell all the maize and cattle that it could produce at the high domestic price. As yet the nascent domestic manufacturing sector showed little sign of expanding to meet the requirements of the mining industry.

In the mining and railway sectors, European workers had succeeded in entrenching themselves in skilled employment by establishing closed-shop trade unions, and then insisting upon 'equal pay for equal work'. In commercial agriculture, European farmers had created a network of price and marketing controls which discriminated against African farmers, either on the grounds of quality (where, as with cattle, African farmers tended to supply lower quality products[14]), or failing that (as in the case of maize) on the unproven grounds that an equally high price for European and African farmers would encourage Africans to exhaust the soil. European wage levels were around 50 times as high as those of African workers in the same sectors. The copper mines, however, had a slightly narrower differential than other sectors between the wages paid to workers of different races, and had already assumed their subsequent role as the highest paying of all major employers.

By 1938, one might claim that the pattern of employment, earnings and economic development that was to characterise much of the next 25 years of Northern Rhodesia's history had already been established. Accordingly, it would be valuable to describe in some detail the pattern of income distribution and employment which prevailed at that time, to offer a standard against which future changes can be compared. Fortunately, Northern Rhodesia was the first country chosen by Phyllis

Table 1.3: Incomes by Sector, 1938 (£000)

	European and Asian			African		
Sector	Resident individuals[a]	Foreigners and foreign companies	Resident companies	Subsistence	Economic	Total taxable incomes[b]
Mining	1,645	4,869	78	–	761	7,353
European agriculture	127	–	–	–	70	197
African agriculture	–	–	–	1,575	228	1,803
African industry	–	–	–	70	36	105
Sawmills and secondary industries	70	–	57	10	48	185
Distribution and transport	978	507	133	–	193	1,811
Others	1,022	275	35	–	402	1,909
Total	3,842	5,651	303	1,655	1,738	13,363

[a]Included in this column are £74,000 of Asian incomes, nearly all in the Distribution sector.
[b]This includes £175,000 of government income.
Source: Deane, *Measurement of Colonial National Incomes*, Table 37, p. 61.

Deane for her pioneering works on national income accounting,[15] and thus there are some remarkably well researched data available for our base year.

Miss Deane's breakdown of 1938 Northern Rhodesian net domestic product (NDP) at factor cost is given in Table 1.3, page 21. In it one is struck by the predominant role played by the mining industry in the economy. Fifty-five per cent of NDP originated in that one sctor, as against only 13.5 per cent for all agriculture, commercial as well as subsistence. Within the mining sector, an extremely large part of revenue accrued as gross operating surpluses to foreign companies: £4,869,000 out of total receipts in 1938 of £10,684,000. A small part of this was paid to the Northern Rhodesian Government in tax, but the final distribution of gross receipts was post-tax profits 39.5 per cent; tax 6.1 per cent; European miners' earnings 15.4 per cent; African miners' earnings 7.1 per cent; and cost of intermediate inputs the remaining 31.9 per cent. By any standards, with a capital/gross output ratio of around 2, the profits received represent a very handsome return on capital.

Outside the mining, agricultural and transport sectors, the economy was scarcely developed. European industry consisted largely of one firm, Zambezi Sawmills, with two-thirds of the sector's entire net output. African industrial output was considered to consist mainly of fishing, beermaking and arts and crafts, the net output of each being valued at £30,000-£40,000 annually.

Miss Deane's figures, implying a value of national income of £8.5 million, contain a sizable margin of error; but the highly concentrated nature of the control of resources in the modern sector meant that the margin of error in estimates of modern sector incomes was small. The main difficulties in estimation arose in connection with subsistence agriculture, for which Miss Deane calculated the value of production in each province on the basis of an estimate of local market prices, although it was found that the final imputed value of subsistence production would have differed only slightly if all output had been valued at Lusaka market prices.

In the economy as a whole, earnings were very unevenly distributed between the races and, within each racial group, between the sectors. Deane's employment and earnings statistics are summarised in Table 1.4, page 23. From this table, if we treat each worker as earning the average income for his racial group in that sector (in other words, if we suppose that each of the 22,900 African selfemployed cash workers receives £9.2, and that each of the 750 European railway workers receives £500),

Table 1.4: Distribution of Employment and Earnings, 1938

Sector	European		African	
	Equivalent annual employment[a]	Average annual earnings (£)	Equivalent annual employment[a]	Average annual earnings (£)[b]
Mining	2,730	662.6	23,750	32.0
European agriculture	350	328.6	12,830	5.4
Government service	655	661.0	5,330	11.0
Railways	750	500.0	6,280	11.6
Cash earnings African commercial farmers	–	–	37,900	3.1[c]
Selfemployed African cash workers	–	–	22,900	9.2
Subsistence agriculture	–	–	302,000	4.6
Total wage economy	6,690	520.6	76,550	15.9

[a] African data were available only in terms of months worked. These have been divided by 12 to produce an 'equivalent annual figure'.
[b] Africans appear on average to have worked only 9 months of the year. True average earnings per worker should be three-quarters of the figure in this column. The employment figures for Africans should be multiplied by 4/3 to arrive at the numbers taking wage employment in a year.
[c] This measured only the value of cash earnings of African commercial farmers and ignored subsistence production by these farmers.
Source: Deane, *Measurement of Colonial National Incomes*, pp. 25-44.

we can derive the Lorenz curve depicted in Figure 1.1, below, in which the cumulative frequency of national earnings is plotted against the cumulative frequency of the work force, ranked in order of decreasing incomes.

Figure 1.1: Lorenz Curve of Income Distribution, 1938

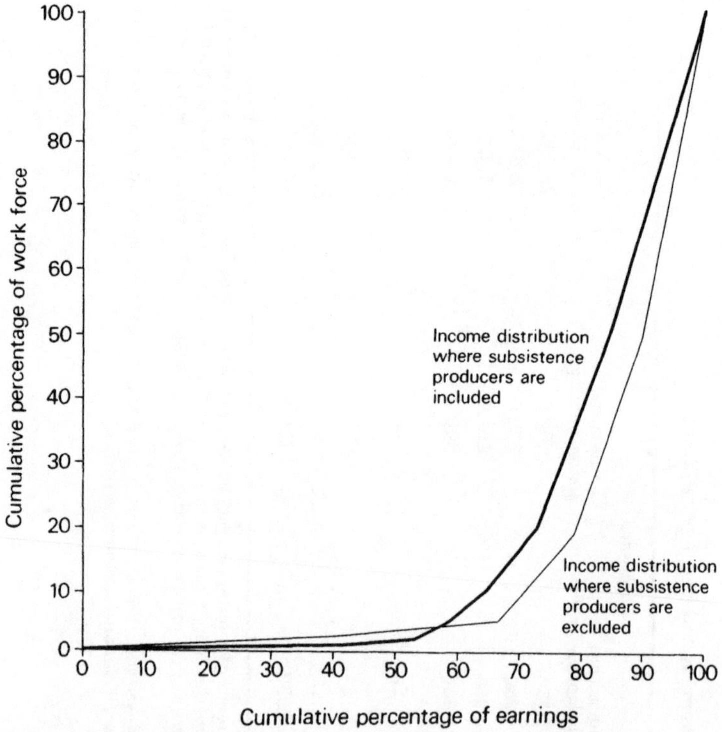

*The only rent, interest or profit incomes included in this measure of earnings are those received by members of the local labour force. Thus non-residents' earnings are excluded.

The basic conclusion to be drawn from Figure 1.1, that income inequality in 1938 was extreme, is undoubtedly valid. However, there are two reasons for supposing that the Lorenz curves in the diagram may exaggerate the degree of inequality. The first is the well known criticism that, by deriving estimates of subsistence incomes which impute a low value to labour time used in the provision of services such as housing and then comparing these estimates with the incomes of modern sector workers who have to purchase all services, one is likely to overstate the differences in living standards. By using a very low valuation of labour time in subsistence households, one implies that a conventional thatched house in traditional society is worth only a fraction of 1 per cent of a European worker's house, a disparity which is much greater than most people's subjective valuation would suggest.

The second reason for taking care in interpreting the Lorenz curves is that at least as many Northern Rhodesians were in wage employment outside the country in 1938 as were employed within the country. Their remittances to, and the agricultural production of, their families in the rural areas of Northern Rhodesia are included in Deane's estimates, but the earnings of members of the household outside the country are excluded if they were not remitted to Northern Rhodesia. The omission of such external earnings will cause our Lorenz curves to overstate the inequality of incomes among Northern Rhodesian households.

With these criticisms in mind, we present two Lorenz curves, (i) where subsistence producers are included, and (ii) where subsistence households (some of whose members may be working outside the country) are excluded. The main percentages to note in connection with the curves are the following:

Cumulative percentage of labour force		0.5	1	2	5	10	20	50
Cumulative percentage of earnings	(i)	22	42	53	59	65	72	84
	(ii)	10	20	40	67	71	79	90

Where subsistence households are included in the total labour force, we observe that the richest 0.5 per cent of the work force earned 22 per cent of the entire earnings of all workers then in Northern Rhodesia. The richest 1 per cent accounted for a remarkable 42 per cent of all earnings; while the top 5 per cent took a full 59 per cent of the total.

By 1938 the future pattern of inequality in racial and sectoral earnings had become established within the domestic economy. In addition, it had emerged and persisted just as clearly in regional development. Certain provinces – those along the line of rail, and the Copperbelt in particular – had become centres of employment, while others had become virtually labour reserves. The Pim Commission estimated the percentage of adult males normally absent from their homes in the different provinces as follows: Eastern Province 50-60 per cent, Barotseland 40-50 per cent, Northern and Luapula Provinces 40 per cent, while the remaining North Western, Copperbelt, Central and Southern Provinces all averaged around 20 per cent.[16] There was considerable variation between districts, ranging from 5 per cent in Livingstone to 70 per cent in Mporokoso in Northern Province.

A clear migration pattern had established itself by this time. Workers from Northern, Luapula and North Western Provinces migrated mainly to the Copperbelt, although the Congo was the destination for a minority, and a few from Northern Province went to work in Tanganyika. Workers in Barotseland went mainly south to Southern Rhodesia or South Africa, though a good number went to the copper mines. Central and Southern Province migrants were evenly divided between nearby towns and commercial farms along the railway line, and Southern Rhodesia; while Eastern Province tax payers tended to prefer Southern Rhodesia.

Although migration continued, the urban population was becoming less migrant in character. Godfrey Wilson's famous study of the African work force in Broken Hill (the present day Kabwe) is generally believed to have overstated the proportion of workers whom he classified as 'temporarily urbanised'—in the sense of having spent in towns over two-thirds of the time since they first left their villages; yet, if we examine both Wilson's results and J. Clyde Mitchell's similar surveys of Luanshya, one decade later, we observe that a sizable proportion of the urban population of the 1940s was committed to an urban life. In Table 1.5, below, Wilson's and Mitchell's results are summarised.

Table 1.5: Characteristics of Adult Male Labour Force

	Permanently urbanised (%)	Temporarily urbanised (%)	Migrant labourers (%)	Peasant visitors (%)
Proportion of working life spent in towns	100	Over 66	33-66	Under 33
Area				
Roan Antelope Mine Township (1951)	11.8	17.7	33.3	37.1
Other Luanshya townships (1951)	26.3	19.6	30.0	23.9
Broken Hill (1940)	1.0	69.9	20.5	8.6

Sources: G. Wilson, *An Essay on the Economics of Detribalisation in Northern Rhodesia*, Part 1 (Rhodes-Livingstone Paper No. 5, 1941); and J.C. Mitchell, *African Urbanisation in Ndola and Luanshya* (Rhodes-Livingstone Communication 6, 1951).

With the increased urbanisation of the population, village relatives enjoyed less pull on the earnings of workers who had migrated. In 1931 Austin Robinson estimated that workers at Roan Antelope mine transferred to the rural areas as much as half their cash earnings. By 1940, Wilson recorded that the proportion remitted from Broken Hill had fallen to 17.7 per cent, mainly in the form of cloth. Despite the trauma of the Depression and the subsequent dismissal of numbers of workers, urban workers were becoming increasingly dependent on urban society for all their needs. One response was to reduce their personal 'social security payment' to their home areas, which they had hoped would provide for them in sickness or old age.

The final feature of the economy in 1938 which is worthy of special note is the growing class consciousness of urban workers, culminating in the 1935 Copperbelt strike and the better organised 1940 strikes. As workers came to view urban wage employment as an attractive alternative to production in the traditional sector, it was inevitable that, while their commitment to rural society diminished, their involvement in activity appropriate to the industrial society in which they had chosen to remain would increase. The 1935 and 1940 strikes were symptoms of the changing perspective of African workers.

Notes

1. NW/A/2/1/2, National Archives, Lusaka: Carden (Acting Administrator, N.W. Rhodesia) to High Commissioner for South Africa, 12 March 1910, quoted in I. Henderson, 'Labour and politics in Northern Rhodesia, 1900-1935: a study in the limits of colonial power' (University of Edinburgh, unpublished PhD thesis, 1972).

2. G. Arrighi, 'Labour Supplies in Historical Perspective: A Study of the Proletarianization of the African Peasantry in Rhodesia', *Journal of Development Studies*, April (1970), pp. 197-234.

3. W.J. Barber, *The Economy of British Central Africa* (Oxford University Press, London, 1961), Ch. VIII.

4. Barber, *Economy of British Central Africa*, pp. 184-6.

5. See, for example, the discussion of the 1918-19 famine in the East Luangwa District in Henderson, 'Labour and politics in Northern Rhodesia'.

6. The validity of the estimate of 50 per cent absence of adult males proving to be the crucial level for 'the integrity of the indigenous economy' may be gauged from a comparison with the figure of only a 5 per cent absence rate from remote districts of Katanga that the Katangese colonial authorities, operating under almost identical conditions to their Northern Rhodesian counterparts, held to be the maximum that 'could be removed from their villages without gravely disturbing the economic and social balance of the community', Richard Gray, *The Two Nations* (Oxford University Press, London, 1960), p. 115.

7. C. van Onselen, 'Worker Consciousness in Black Miners: Southern Rhodesia 1900-1920', *Journal of African History*, vol. XIV(2), (1973), pp. 239-42.

8. Audrey Richards, *Land, Labour and Diet in Northern Rhodesia* (Oxford University Press, London, 1939), see pp. 40 and 399; and Betty Preston Thompson, *Two Studies in African Nutrition* (Rhodes-Livingstone Paper 24, 1954).

9. R.E. Baldwin, *Economic Development and Export Growth: A Study of Northern Rhodesia, 1920-1960* (University of California Press, Los Angeles, 1966), p. 84.

10. See Arrighi, *Labour Supplies*, p. 211.

11. In 1935, 11 per cent of tax obligations were discharged in this manner.

12. Note that the copper mines' understanding of 'stabilisation' differed somewhat from the meaning more commonly found in sociological theory. Whereas sociologists speak of workers being stabilised in towns only when workers spend the rest of their natural lives in towns, the copper mines made it clear on many occasions that they wanted workers to remain in town only during their working lifetimes. The provision of many social services, and of a house and income after retirement, were held to be the responsibility of traditional society.

13. E.A.G. Robinson, 'The Organisation of African Mine Workers', Ch. X, in J. Merle Davis (ed.), *Modern Industry and the African* (Frank Cass, London, 1967), pp. 173-4.

14. In the case of cattle, import controls were manipulated to encourage the importation of low-grade beef, while restricting the importation of prime cattle. Between 1937 and 1956, the producer price of prime cattle rose 460 per cent, compared with a rise of only 200 per cent for lower quality animals. See Baldwin, *Economic Development and Export Growth*, p. 158.

15. P. Deane, *The Measurement of Colonial National Incomes: An Experiment*, National Institute of Economic and Social Research (NIESR), Occasional Paper XII (Cambridge University Press, London, 1948), and *Colonial Social Accounting* (NIESR, London, 1953).

16. *Report of the Commission appointed to Inquire into the Financial and Economic Position of Northern Rhodesia*, Col. No. 145 (HMSO, London, 1938), p. 36.

2 BEFORE INDEPENDENCE

Second World War

The Second World War years saw a consolidation of the erratic growth of the 1930s. Some Northern Rhodesians were employed as *askaris* in the Middle and Far Eastern battle zones, but the most significant impact of the war on the economy was to provide a breathing space in which sectors supplying mining inputs could gear themselves up to the high persistent demand from the mines.

Copper production varied surprisingly little during the war years, since the mines were constrained by a lack of essential skilled labour, raw materials and capital. Yet employment on the mines rose steadily because new development work was encouraged, and in 1940, both African and European miners were successful in using strike action to bring the monetary and real values of their cash earnings back to the levels prevailing ten years earlier. Furthermore, the shortage of skilled workers was so great that, for the duration of the war only, Africans were permitted to carry out some 'European' jobs. While copper output changed little, other sectors grew rapidly. The money value of European and African agricultural net output in 1945 was three times as large as in 1938. The growth of manufacturing output was even faster.

After the war, as shortages eased, the mining industry was able to expand again to take advantage of rising world copper demand and rising copper prices. A comparison of the situations in 1938, 1945 and 1948 is given in Table 2.1, below. The boom in copper prices and the

Table 2.1: National Income, 1938-48*

Territorial output by sectors	1938 (£m)	%	1945 (£m)	%	1948 (£m)	%
Mining	7.4	54.8	7.4	33.6	18.5	47.4
Commercial agriculture and livestock	0.4	3.0	1.2	5.5	1.7	4.9
Forestry, manufacture, building	0.3	2.2	1.4	6.4	2.7	6.9
African village industry	0.2	1.5	0.9	4.1	0.9	2.3
Distribution and transport	1.8	13.4	3.2	14.5	5.7	14.6
Government	0.9	6.7	1.6	7.3	2.5	6.4

Territorial output by sectors	1938 (£m)	%	1945 (£m)	%	1948 (£m)	%
Subsistence agriculture	1.6	11.8	4.4	20.0	4.5	11.0
Other	0.9	6.6	1.9	8.6	2.5	6.4
Total territorial output	13.5	100.0	22.0	100.0	39.0	100.0
Territorial incomes						
Non-African individuals	3.9	28.9	6.0	27.3	10.7	27.5
Africans	3.5	25.2	10.3	46.8	11.5	29.5
Companies	6.0	44.4	5.4	24.5	16.4	42.0
Government	0.2	1.5	0.3	1.4	0.4	1.0
NDP						
(Total geographical product)	13.6	100.0	22.0	100.0	39.0	100.0
NNP	8.5		18.5		25.5	

*Values in £m at current prices.
Source: P. Deane, *Colonial Social Accounting* (National Institute of Economic and Social Research, London, 1953), pp. 63-7; and *National Income and Social Accounts of Northern Rhodesia, 1945-1953* (Central Statistical Office, Lusaka, 1964), Table 1.

return of European miners from military service can be seen to account for distributional shifts between 1945 and 1948 which almost exactly offset the shifts that occurred between 1938 and 1945. It has proved impossible to construct a consistent table from Miss Deane's work on the 1945 data to correspond to Table 1.3 of Chapter 1, but it is possible to produce figures for 1945 that correspond to Table 1.4 and the Lorenz curves (Figure 1.1) for 1938. The 1945 data are given in Table 2.2, below, and Figure 2.1, page 31. Some of the main percentages to note in con-

Table 2.2: Distribution of Employment and Earnings, 1945

	European		African	
Sector	Annual employment	Average annual earnings (£)	Annual employment	Average annual earnings (£)
Mining	3,525	737	33,000	41.2
European agriculture	NA	NA	27,000	10.3
Government service	1,070	606	29,700	18.9
Railways and transport	736	580	5,400	17.1

	European		African	
Sector	Annual employment	Average annual earnings (£)	Annual employment	Average annual earnings (£)
Cash earnings				
African commercial farmers	–	–	60,000	10.0
Self-employed African cash workers	–	–	39,000	13.5
Subsistence agriculture	–	–	400,000	11.4
Total wage economy	8,841	612	142,300	21.8

Source: Deane, *Colonial Social Accounting*, pp. 27 and 243.

Figure 2.1: Lorenz Curve of Income Distribution, 1945

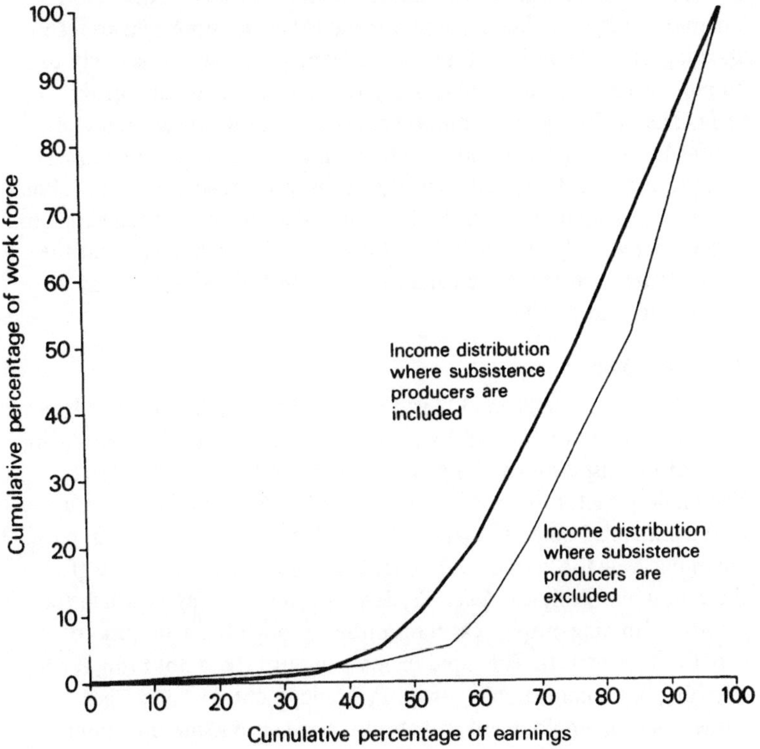

*The only rent, interest or profit incomes included in this measure of earnings are those received by members of the local labour force. Thus non-residents' earnings are excluded.

nection with Figure 2.1 are the following:

Cumulative percentage of the labour force:										
	0.25	0.5	0.75	1	1.5	2	5	10	20	50
Cumulative percentage of earnings:										
(i)	16	23	30	35	37	39	45	51	60	76
(ii)	11	18	23	28	35	42	56	61	69	84

Thus it would appear that, where subsistence households are included in the total labour force, the richest 0.5 per cent in 1945 earned 23 per cent of total national earnings (as against 22 per cent in 1938); the richest 1 per cent accounted for 35 per cent of the total (as against 42 per cent); and the richest 5 per cent took 45 per cent (as against 59 per cent).

Since Figure 2.1 was constructed from much more detailed statistics on income distribution at high income levels than was Figure 1.1 of Chapter 1, page 24 (being based, for non-Africans, upon census returns showing the distribution of incomes by income classes), it is likely to be more accurate in describing distribution at the upper end of the scale. The qualifications expressed above, as regards the accuracy of Figure 1.1 as a representation of income inequality, apply with equal force to Figure 2.1. Nonetheless, the difference between Figures 1.1 and 2.1 is so great that we might fairly assume that income inequalities diminished between 1938 and 1945, although Table 2.1 suggests that the improvement was short lived and that, by 1948, the situation had reverted to that of 1938.

Post-War Boom

The period after the Second World War until the establishment of the Federation of Rhodesia and Nyasaland in 1953 witnessed an entrenchment of the disparities and inequalities observed in 1938 and 1945. The modern sector of the economy expanded enormously as a result of the minerals boom associated with the Korean War. Table 2.3, page 33, illustrates how the various components of national income grew after the war, while Table 2.4, page 33, demonstrates the way in which the growth of mining output was transmitted through the economy to benefit other sectors. The rapid increase in output did not bring forth anything like a comparable growth in employment. Detailed data on modern sector employment and average earnings outside the mining sector are sadly lacking for this period, but such data as exist are summarised in Tables 2.5 and 2.6, pages 34 and 35.

Table 2.3: Growth of Components of National Income after 1945*

Sectors	1945	1947	1949 (£m)	1951	1953
Non-African wages and salaries and income from unincorporated enterprises	6.1	8.4	13.1	19.5	28.6
African wages and salaries and income from unincorporated enterprises	3.3	4.2	6.6	11.4	22.1
Mining companies' incomes and royalties	3.1	11.4	19.1	47.6	52.9
Other companies' incomes	1.0	1.3	1.6	2.4	3.2
Net domestic output	13.7	25.5	41.0	81.4	107.7
Less net interest, dividends and profits remitted abroad	2.3	10.3	13.6	27.2	24.0
Net national income in money economy	11.4	15.2	27.4	54.2	83.7

*Values in £m at current prices. Note: these figures apply only to the monetary economy. The CSO estimated subsistence output at a nominal £5 million per annum throughout this period.

Source: *National Income and Social Accounts of Northern Rhodesia, 1945-1953*, (Central Statistical Office, Lusaka), Table 1, p. 23.

Table 2.4: Domestic (Monetary) Output by Industrial Origin*

Industry	1945	1947	1949 (£m)	1951	1953
Mining	7.6	16.8	26.8	59.7	69.7
Central and local government	1.1	1.8	2.9	5.2	9.8
Railways	0.9	0.8	1.2	1.7	2.7
Wholesale and retail trade	1.3	2.2	3.4	5.1	8.5
European agriculture	0.8	1.0	1.3	2.1	2.5
Other industries	2.0	2.9	5.4	7.6	14.5
Total	13.7	25.5	41.0	81.4	107.7

*Values in £m at current prices.

Source: *National Income and Social Accounts of Northern Rhodesia, 1945-1953*, Table 16, p. 38.

Table 2.5: Wage Employment by Race and by Sector

Sector	1945		1949		1951		1953	
	African	Non-African	African	Non-African	African	Non-African	African	Non-African
Agriculture	27,000	700	32,400*	509	37,000	1,000	39,000+	460+
Construction	6,000	150	21,020	500	46,000	700	56,000	3,200+
Domestic service	17,500	–	23,000	–	30,250	–	35,700	–
Government	29,700	1,070	NA	NA	NA	2,750	32,000	4,500
Mines	33,000	3,525	37,220	4,746	42,150	6,170	46,100	6,950
Transport	5,400	736	7,106	445	7,400	1,630	8,150	2,005
Total	142,300	8,841	172,000*	10,878	228,251	15,992	240,000+	20,900

*These are 1947 figures, the 1949 statistics being unavailable.
+These are 1954 figures, the 1953 statistics being unavailable.

Source: *Labour Department, Annual Reports, 1945-1954,* Statistical Appendices; Deane, *Colonial Social Accounting*, pp. 27 and 243; *Central African Territories: Geographical, Historical and Economic Survey*, Cmnd 8234 (HMSO, London, 1951), Appendix 2; *The African Native Market in the Federation of Rhodesia and Nyasaland*, Board of Trade (HMSO, London, 1954), p. 3; and *Manpower Report* (Government Printer, Lusaka, 1966), Table B-4.

Table 2.6: Average Earnings by Race (£ per annum)

Class of worker	1938	1945	1947	1949	1951	1953
African miners (money wages + copper bonus + rations)	24	33	38	52	78	124
African miners' earnings (at 1939 prices)	23	19	19	25	35	51
European miners (total money earnings)	663	737	1,023	1,056	1,275	1,782
European miners' earnings (at 1939 prices)	672	581	750	707	789	911
African agricultural workers (money wage)*	5.4	10	18	36	28	26
African wage workers (money earnings)	16	22	NA	44	47	77
European wage workers (money earnings)	521	612	NA	998	1,030	1,191

*Agriculture employment and earnings statistics are acknowledged to be extremely unreliable.

Source: *National Accounts 1945-1953*, p. 39; Deane's data analysed in Tables 2.5 and 2.8 of this chapter; R.E. Baldwin, *Economic Development and Export Growth: A Study of Northern Rhodesia, 1920-1960* (University of California Press, Los Angeles, 1966), pp. 87-90; and calculations made from these references.

In the urban sector, this immediate postwar era might be interpreted as marking the turning point in the economy's transition from a low wage-low efficiency to a high wage-high efficiency situation. The stabilisation of the African labour force on the mines continued steadily, so that by 1951, 67 per cent of African mine workers at one large mine were living with their families in the mine townships, with a further 14 per cent unmarried,[1] and by 1958 the figure for those married and with their families was 84 per cent. Labour turnover continued to fall. From 83 per cent per annum at Roan Antelope in 1938, the figure fell to 77 per cent in 1947, 24 per cent in 1952 and 20 per cent in 1958. At the same time the ratio of African wages to European wages and to equipment costs started to rise, and labour-substituting mechanisation (requiring both relatively more machines and relatively more skilled workers, to man the machines, per unit of output) occurred on a significant scale. Between 1947 and 1958, for example, whereas equipment costs rose by about 100 per cent, African and European earnings rose by 344 and 66 per cent respectively.[2] As a result, the African and European labour coefficients per tonne of copper changed from 0.162 and 0.0182 to 0.088 and 0.0180 respectively.

The cause of the unprecedented rise in African earnings on the mines—a phenomenon that was repeated throughout the economy—did not lie in a sudden shortage of labour seeking employment on the mines. A labour shortage did emerge briefly in 1950,[3] but on the whole there was no problem of finding sufficient numbers of recruits for unskilled mining jobs.[4] The reason for the rise seemed to lie much more in a complex interaction of institutional-cum-racial and economic factors.

To take the more directly economic factors first, the mines were still actively pursuing a policy of stabilisation, in the hope of raising labour efficiency further. The benefits from stabilisation were related directly to maintaining, or, if possible, reducing, the already low level of labour turnover, which, in turn, depended upon ensuring that employment in copper mining remained more attractive than employment elsewhere. As competing sectors of wage employment grew in size, and threatened to attract men away from the mines, it was not sufficient merely for the mines to provide good living conditions for their workers. They also had to offer better wages if their labour force was to remain stable.

Analysing the situation in terms of the economy as a whole, the supply of labour had ceased to be perfectly elastic at a near-subsistence wage rate. In part this was owing to a reluctance by District Officers to collect taxes with as much force as was the case in the first 30 years of the century. The tax weapon was used to coerce labour during national emergencies such as the Second World War, but otherwise it was not a major instrument of labour policy. Furthermore, with the advent of the Labour Party to power in Britain in 1945, the colonial authorities ended their earlier opposition to the formation of African workers' organisations. This change in policy was hardly compatible with continued attempts at the coercion of labour.

Employers probably were not wholly unhappy that an unlimited supply of labour was not available at low wage rates. Even without the authorities forcing workers into seeking wage employment, there were social and political problems related to the numbers of unemployed Africans in the towns. The coercion of labour would only aggravate the situation. In addition, the advantages accruing to employers from stabilisation depended upon labour remaining willingly in its employment. Thus, a rising demand for labour was met through raising real wages. And, if the copper mines wished to maintain their privileged position in the labour market, they had to be sure that their terms of employment remained more attractive than those of their main rivals in the domestic economy.

The other important economic factor at work arose directly out of the higher wages that were paid to Africans. As African workers became more expensive factors of production, increasing attention was paid by employers to making more efficient use of them. One point of view that became popular among employers was that, in terms of infrastructural (e.g. housing, health facilities) and training expenditure, they had already made large investments in their African work force. The marginal rates of return from extra investments in training could be very high indeed. But this was where institutional/racial factors intervened. For the jobs that seemed ideally suited to African workers with some extra training were jobs which were reserved for (European) members of the Northern Rhodesia Mineworkers' Union (NRMWU). African advancement into these grades of employment depended upon some accommodation being reached between the NRMWU and the mining companies.

During the era of high mining profits which lasted up until 1953, it would have been very costly for the mines to risk a confrontation with either of the main groups of employees, and they acquired relative industrial peace only at the price of large pay rises to both European and African workers. African workers fared particularly well, since they now had the advantage of a trade union of their own, the Northern Rhodesia African Mine Workers Union (NRAMU), formed in 1949 under the leadership of Lawrence Katilungu. With the union to pursue their claims they managed to make up some of the leeway on European miners that their weak bargaining position had cost them before. In particular, African miners gained from the extension to them of the copper bonus scheme granted to European miners, relating bonuses to copper mining profits. When copper prices fell after 1953, the potential cost of a strike to copper mining profits was somewhat reduced, while the risk to employees' future employment in the event of striking was greater; and the gain in profits from advancing low-paid Africans into former 'European' jobs came to look more attractive. So it was that, in 1955, the first agreement for African advancement was signed between the mining companies and the NRMWU.

Although African advancement did not actually occur until 1955, it would not be fanciful to suggest that the certainty of its arrival influenced the trend of African wages before 1953. The issue of African advancement focused attention upon those grades of employment that might be opened up to African workers, and it became readily apparent that, if the African pay scale were to be extended upward to include the jobs open for advancement, a very considerable gap would exist between European and African earnings in those grades – this being, of course, one of the main reasons why the copper companies favoured African advancement. At this point the racially divided nature of the trade union movement and of job demarcation impinged upon the scene. The Europeans in the NRMWU refused to entertain any reduction in the earnings of Europeans in the jobs into which Africans were to advance, for they could see that these jobs were merely the thin edge of the wedge of African advancement. The Africans in the NRAMU were unwilling to approve any wage differential between the races that was larger than that which could be justified as necessary extra costs of expatriates. Furthermore, they were opposed to any move which separated the wage rates paid to Africans in the 'advanced' jobs from those in other employment grades. The mining companies attempted later to divide the African workers by creating a separate union, the Mines African Staff Association, to cater only for senior African employees. But there can be little doubt that the general impact of African advancement upon wage scales, given the downward inflexibility of European wages, was to raise the average level of African wages, with some of the upward adjustment occurring even before 1953.[5]

In as much as most other sectors benefited considerably from the copper boom, they were able to give their African workers large pay increases and preserve relative differentials. However, old habits die hard and, in commercial agriculture in particular, some employers continued to prefer to rely upon a mixture of low wages and coercion as a means of acquiring a labour force. Throughout the 1940s, Labour Department Annual Reports refer to monthly wages of 6s 0d-8s 0d (30p-40p) being paid to agricultural workers on many European farms, and the reports mention how the farmers would complain of the low efficiency of the workers and of a labour shortage. The low efficiency was hardly surprising when one learns that the Poverty Datum Line for a married man plus two children was estimated in Livingstone in 1941 at 57s 0d (£2.85p) a month.[6] But, rather than tackle the shortage and low efficiency problems direct by raising wages, many farmers preferred to use conscription, recruitment agencies or a new institution, the African Labour Corps, to solve their labour difficulties.

During the Second World War the government was able, and willing, to use its powers of conscription to draft large numbers of labourers to European farms. These powers lapsed at the end of the war, but alternative, government-subsidised forms of creating a labour supply emerged. The government Controller of African Recruitment organised large-scale recruitment, effectively subsidising farmers to the tune of 6s 0d (30p) per recruit per month. In 1943, a 630-strong African Labour Corps was established, on military lines, to provide disciplined workers for farmers on a 50 per cent subsidised basis.[7] But agricultural labour shortages persisted, and were aggravated when minimum wage regulations in other sectors started to appear, fixing wages elsewhere much above those in agriculture. In 1950, an agricultural recruitment agency was set up to try to direct potential workers from the poorest regions of Northern Rhodesia, Nyasaland and Tanganyika into agricultural employment. Although most farmers along the line of rail had, by 1953, come to prefer a more efficient, more expensive, work force, and as a result, the average level of agricultural wages in 1953 was much above that in 1945, a sizable number of European farmers continued to rely largely upon a foreign recruited labour force for their cheap labour needs.[8]

Agriculture was not bypassed by the boom conditions after the war. Maize and virginia tobacco production rose two- or threefold between 1945 and 1953, and no market constraint intervened, the tobacco all going for export and the maize still proving insufficient for local demand. European farmers maintained their predominant position in commercial production and continued their discrimination against African maize and cattle producers. But, even so, African maize sales grew faster than those by European farmers. The exact nature of the discrimination altered in the case of maize, becoming based more upon the techniques of production employed than upon the race of the farmer. The discrimination practised by the Cattle Control Board, however, continued as before.

In maize pricing policy, the first innovation, after the establishment in 1936 of the Maize Control Board, came in 1943, when the board, using government subsidies, deliberately chose to pursue a policy of holding down labour costs to employers. From that year until 1954, the country had to import maize, but the board fixed the producer and selling prices in such a way that the import prices were greater than the European producer price, which was, in turn, greater than the African producer price, which exceeded the selling price. During these years £7 million was spent to keep down the costs of industrial labour, while, in the meantime, producers' incomes were held down below the levels that would have prevailed with a free market.[9]

The situation became even more complicated in 1949, when the Maize Control Board accepted the logic of its earlier criticisms of the environmental impact of African commercial farming and introduced the African Farming Improvement Scheme. A pilot scheme of 'African improved farmers' was commenced in 1946 in Southern Province, paying higher prices to African farmers who adopted approved conservationist methods of farming maize.[10] This scheme proved sufficiently successful for the authorities, in 1949, to extend it to cover the entire country. For the next decade or so, two prices were paid to African maize farmers. 'Unimproved' farmers received 20 to 25 per cent below the price paid to European producers, while 'improved' farmers received a bonus based upon acreage to bring prices up to those paid to Europeans.

Despite this gesture towards African farmers, a gesture which tended to benefit those farmers who were already more than usually prosperous, the bulk of African agriculture remained neglected when compared with European production. Marketing was directed towards European producers, forcing Africans to pay high transport costs on their deliveries to marketing depots. Extension services remained heavily biased against Africans.[11] The rural road network was most rudimentary. Yet, with the adoption of the plough and other ox-drawn implements, African agriculture was able to expand to a point where farms of 30 acres or more were common in some areas of Southern Province.[12]

In many ways, the 1945-53 period could be typified as one in which the Northern Rhodesian money economy was enlarged by a scale factor, without anything dramatic intervening to upset the underlying structure. Incomes in the money sectors rose everywhere by a substantial amount, yet the institutional factors governing the division of the economy into 'European' and 'African' areas of employment remained little changed. Surprisingly, even the breakdown of the African labour force into rural/urban or wage/non-wage employment changed very little over the period. Kuczynski and Orde Browne[13] estimated that 54.1 per cent of the adult male population was at work for wages in 1937, while the Department of Labour put the proportion at 54.6 per cent in 1951. Yet the stability of structure was deceptive. Urban wage earners were emerging ever more strongly as an economically privileged class, with the ratio of average urban African wages to peasant farmer earnings rising from 1.9 in 1945 to 3.0 in 1953—a rate of divergence reinforced by the government's intervention to hold down the cost of foodstuffs to urban consumers.

Federation

It was only when the copper boom ended at the start of the Federal era in 1953/4 that significant changes could occur in the structure of the work force and in the distribution of income; since it was only then that the mining companies felt able to risk a strike from European mine workers over the companies' desire to advance African workers into 'European' jobs. When copper prices fell, mining profits followed suit, and the relative attraction of substituting cheap African labour for European labour increased, while the chances that a serious strike could precipitate a closure of a mine became more real and acted as a deterrent against strike action. Thus, in 1955, the mining companies renegotiated their agreement with the European union, and the first African advancement agreement was signed, permitting Africans to advance into 30 jobs formerly reserved for Europeans. Around 1,000 Africans benefited from this agreement, and in 1960 another advancement agreement permitted a further 400 Africans to move into 'European' jobs. The impact upon African wages of the advancement of a mere 4 per cent of the African mine labour force into 'European' jobs was considerable, for the mines came to accept demands for the creation of a unified non-racial mine pay scale. Between 1954 and 1962, average African earnings on the mines rose by 124 per cent compared with an increase of only 21 per cent for Europeans. In Tables 2.7-2.9, pages 42-4, the information on output, employment and earnings during the Federation is summarised.

From this mass of statistics several features stand out; the first being that, over the nine years of Federation, African employment, despite the first tentative steps towards African advancement, actually fell, while non-African employment rose by 30 per cent. On closer examination one observes that the fall can be attributed entirely to the rundown of the construction sector, as government and private investment was curtailed during the uncertainty surrounding the breakup of Federation. Large increases in employment actually occurred in the service sectors. Yet the overall trend fairly reflects the pattern of employment in the key productive sectors.

The explanation of the very different employment trends between the races lies in the data given in Tables 2.8 and 2.9. Africans in wage employment during the Federation were able to increase their wages at an average annual rate of 8.5 per cent on the mines, compared with 8.3 per cent for African employees as a whole, while the comparable figures for non-African workers were 2.1 and 2.8 per cent respectively. With higher costs of unskilled labour, employers were encouraged to substitute

Table 2.7: Analysis of GDP at Factor Cost*

	1954	1956	1958	1960	1962
			(£m)		
GDP by categories of income					
Non-African earnings	35.1	46.7	48.4	55.8	57.6
African monetary earnings	20.8	29.6	32.4	37.1	39.4
Rural household consumption	16.7	19.0	20.3	21.5	20.0
Gross operating profits	64.1	90.9	36.6	88.5	74.8
GDP by industrial origin					
Non-African agriculture	2.3	3.2	2.9	4.1	4.9
African agricultural sales	1.5	2.1	1.0	2.2	3.0
Mining	79.2	108.8	51.1	107.3	93.8
Manufacturing	5.1	7.4	8.9	9.5	10.2
Construction	8.9	13.0	14.1	9.6	7.6
African rural household services	3.3	3.7	4.0	4.1	4.0
Other	38.6	53.4	59.9	71.2	74.7
GDP at factor cost	139.9	191.6	141.9	208.8	198.2

*Values in £m at current prices.
Source: *National Accounts of the Federation of Rhodesia and Nyasaland, 1954-1962*, pp. 69-71.

Table 2.8: Employees and Earnings (£ per annum), 1954-63*

Sector		1954	1956	1958	1960	1962	1963
Agriculture	A	39,000	35,200	36,000	37,400	38,700	36,000
	A	(41)	(45)	(55)	(60)	(64)	(66)
	N-A	460	400	600	740	660	700
	N-A	(803)	(1,032)	(1,128)	(1,203)	(1,230)	(1,325)
Mining	A	44,100	46,200	39,900	42,700	41,100	40,800
	A	(132)	(184)	(231)	(285)	(296)	(298)
	N-A	6,840	7,730	7,380	8,030	8,330	8,230
	N-A	(2,120)	(2,429)	(2,196)	(2,594)	(2,563)	(2,575)
Manufacturing	A	16,100	17,300	18,500	17,900	17,400	15,900
	A	(76)	(97)	(101)	(118)	(142)	(173)
	N-A	1,710	1,880	2,200	2,640	2,880	2,980
	N-A	(1,080)	(1,177)	(1,257)	(1,330)	(1,342)	(1,352)

Sector		1954	1956	1958	1960	1962	1963
Construction	A	56,000	65,000	62,000	36,000	23,900	23,400
	A	(74)	(96)	(106)	(118)	(127)	(138)
	N-A	3,200	3,900	4,240	2,730	1,900	1,880
	N-A	(1,094)	(1,338)	(1,368)	(1,438)	(1,420)	(1,470)
Services	A	63,600	73,500	78,200	82,000	82,400	84,200
	A	(66)	(81)	(96)	(107)	(124)	(134)
	N-A	5,680	6,550	7,860	8,760	9,320	9,180
	N-A	(829)	(959)	(1,080)	(1,151)	(1,194)	(1,228)
Other	A	21,600	25,400	26,200	27,800	27,300	24,200
	A	(76)	(94)	(112)	(126)	(164)	(174)
	N-A	6,880	8,620	9,770	10,110	10,210	9,520
	N-A	(839)	(912)	(987)	(1,093)	(1,149)	(1,195)
Total	A	240,000	263,000	261,000	244,000	231,000	225,000
	A	(78)	(100)	(115)	(136)	(151)	(160)
	N-A	24,800	29,100	32,100	33,000	33,300	31,700
	N-A	(1,237)	(1,400)	(1,356)	(1,523)	(1,548)	(1,585)

*Earnings are in parentheses. A=Africans; N-A=Non-Africans.
Source: *Manpower Report* (Government Printer, Lusaka, 1966), Tables B-4, B-5.

machines and skilled labour for unskilled (largely African) workers. Indeed Table 2.9 suggests that, on the copper mines, gains in real wages were almost exactly offset by equivalent relative falls in labour intensity in production.

In the agricultural sector, output continued to expand, and gradually the discrimination against African producers was removed. However, by this time, the structure of production had taken such a form that Europeans had little to fear from competition from African farmers. At the start of the Federal era, a maize export surplus reappeared after 20 years of maize imports. European and 'improved' African farmers were relatively unaffected by the change, since they continued to receive the subsidised producer price, though, whereas before they were receiving less than the import-parity, free market price, now they received more than the export-parity price likely to prevail in free market conditions. The farmers who suffered were the 'unimproved' African farmers, whose levies rose to such a high level that they often actually received less than the 'export-parity minus marketing costs' price that they might have had

Table 2.9: Indices of Output and Real Wage per African Miner, 1956-64*

Year	Index of African mine employment (1)	Index of copper production (2)	Index of copper output per African miner (2)/(1)=3	Index of real wage of an African miner (4)	Index of real labour cost of African miners per unit of copper production (5)=(4)/(3)
1956	100.0	100.0	100.0	100.0	100.0
1957	103.3	108.5	104.8	108.0	102.8
1958	91.3	98.0	107.4	115.8	107.9
1959	87.2	136.7	156.8	128.2	81.8
1960	98.1	145.9	148.7	146.3	98.4
1961	104.0	144.0	138.5	146.6	105.9
1962	100.4	140.9	140.3	136.9	97.5
1963	98.4	146.3	148.6	156.6	105.3
1964	101.5	163.2	160.7	176.4	109.7

*1956=100.0.

Source: Derived from *Report of the Commission of Inquiry into the Mining Industry*, 1966, under the chairmanship of Roland Brown (The Brown Commission Report) (Government Printer, Lusaka, 1966), Appendix XVII, p. 161.

to accept in the old days of the Maize Control Board.[14] In 1957 the export subsidy vanished and the domestic consumer price for maize was increased. The price paid by the Grain Marketing Board to farmers throughout the Federation became a weighted average of the export and domestic consumer price – a move that implied an element of subsidy from Northern Rhodesian to Southern Rhodesian producers.[15] From 1957 to the end of Federation in 1963, pricing policy changed little.

The discriminatory pricing policy on cattle, which had persisted ever since the Cattle Control Board was established in 1937, came to an end in 1960, when freer market conditions were allowed to prevail and the prices for African cattle rose appreciably. But, in the meantime, the relative producer price of maize compared to cattle had doubled for African farmers between 1947 and 1959, and the African share of the cattle market had fallen from 63 per cent in 1944 to 44 per cent in 1960.[16]

Summary

The unequal nature of income distribution in the Northern Rhodesian economy on the eve of its independence emerges clearly from the description presented above. Until the development of the copper mines the inequality was on a racial basis and was of a very pure form, with Africans confined to the role of suppliers of cheap migrant labour, for Southern Rhodesian mines and industries in the main. After the Depression, conditions of employment for African workers improved, as employers found it in their economic interest to try to create a stabilised urban labour force. But the earnings gap between the races was only very slowly reduced. It was only in the decade before independence that it became possible for Africans to enter the range of jobs that had been formerly the preserve of Europeans. The racial inequality of the economy was not confined to earnings and employment differences – differences which were diminishing gradually, as one can see if one compares Figure 2.2, page 46, showing income distribution in 1959, with Figures 1.1 and 2.1, pages 24 and 31. The inequality extended to housing, social and health facilities, and also to the key area of education. This was particularly true in the case of technical education, for Africans were excluded by law from becoming apprentices until 1959. Overall government recurrent expenditure on African education had remained low throughout the colonial period.[17] Before the Second World War, recurrent expenditure on European education exceeded that on African education, and even as late as 1959-60, when £1,844,000 was spent on

Figure 2.2: Lorenz Curves of Income Distribution, 1938, 1945 and 1959*

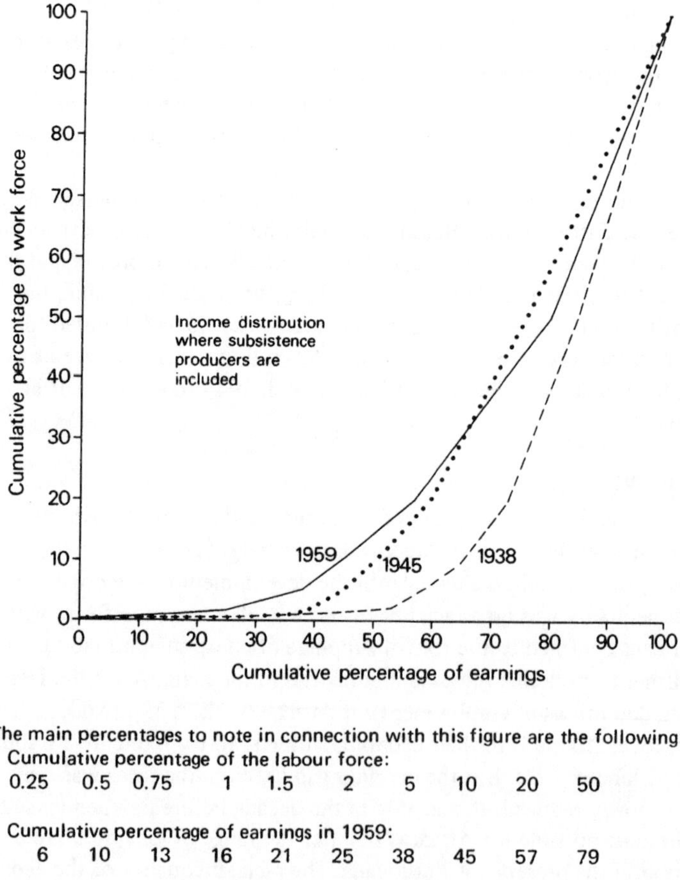

*The main percentages to note in connection with this figure are the following:

Cumulative percentage of the labour force:									
0.25	0.5	0.75	1	1.5	2	5	10	20	50
Cumulative percentage of earnings in 1959:									
6	10	13	16	21	25	38	45	57	79

Source: Baldwin, *Economic Growth*, Tables 2-9, p. 46.

African education, the total spent on European education was nearly as large, being £1,485,000.[18] Yet, at no time in the country's history has the European population exceeded 2 per cent of the national total.

The structure of the educational expenditure was not calculated to alleviate the inequality greatly either. In 1944, 49 out of 102,000 African schoolchildren were in secondary school, and by 1960 the figure had improved merely to 2,600 out of 290,000, with only 28 students in the final year of secondary school.[19] There were only 4 African university graduates in 1951, and, at the start of the year of independence, 1964, the country possessed a total of 961 Africans with secondary school certificates and 76 with university degrees.[20]

Yet, by 1954, another form of inequality had started to trouble policy makers – the inequality between the rural and urban populations, with the latter economically much better off than the former, and with the gap widening fast. Until 1945, the incomes of African urban wage earners were around double those of peasant farmers. With the rapid wage rises of the Korean War copper boom, the ratio had risen to 3 by 1953, and this rate of growth continued unabated till 1963, when the ratio was 5. The discussion in subsequent chapters will be much concerned with this particular form of inequality.

Notes

1. J. C. Mitchell, *African Urbanisation in Ndola and Luanshya* (Rhodes-Livingstone Communication 6, 1951), p. 7, Table V.
2. R. E. Baldwin, *Economic Development and Export Growth: A Study of Northern Rhodesia, 1920-1960* (University of California Press, Los Angeles, 1966), p. 95.
3. *Labour Department Annual Report* (1950), p. 7.
4. If one looks at Table 2.5, there is nothing to suggest that Barber's analysis of the situation in terms of the sudden attainment of 'quasi-full employment' has anything to do with the rapid increase in wage levels. In his terms, employment had been 'quasi-full' long before wages rose in the 1940s; c.f. W.J. Barber, *The Economy of British Central Africa* (Oxford University Press, London, 1961).
5. The advancement of Africans is discussed in detail in Chapters 5 and 6.
6. Unfortunately, the reports give no information as to the components of the Poverty Datum Line estimated in Livingstone. However, even after allowing for the differences in the cost of living between the town and the country, and the free housing and rations given to agricultural labourers, the gap between the real earnings of an agricultural labourer on some farms and the Livingstone Poverty Datum Line would remain substantial – probably equivalent to more than half of the 57s 0d a month.
7. *Labour Department Annual Reports* for 1943, p. 2; for 1946, p. 5; for 1947, pp. 5-6; for 1950, pp. 7-8; and for 1952, p. 6.
8. *Labour Department Annual Report*, 1951, pp. 5-6.
9. Baldwin, *Economic Growth*, pp. 155-6.
10. See C.E. Johnson, 'African Farming Improvement in the Plateau Tonga Maize Areas of Northern Rhodesia', *Agricultural Bulletin No. 11*, Department of Agriculture, (1956), pp. 7-9.
11. See, for example, Barber, *Economy of British Central Africa*, pp. 152-5.
12. Johnson, 'African Farming Improvement', pp. 19-20.
13. R.R. Kuczynski, *Demographic Survey of the British Empire*, vol. ii (London, Oxford University Press, 1949), pp. 462-7; and Major G. St. J. Orde Browne, *Report on Labour Conditions in Northern Rhodesia* (HMSO, London, 1938).
14. Baldwin, *Economic Growth*, pp. 156-7.
15. Baldwin, *Economic Growth*, pp. 156-7.

16. Baldwin, *Economic Growth*, pp. 158-9.

17. For details of educational expenditure see *Manpower Report* (Government Printer, Lusaka, 1966), p. 141.

18. *Manpower Report*; and Baldwin, *Economic Growth*, p. 194.

19. Baldwin, *Economic Growth*, p. 50.

20. *Manpower Report* (1966), pp. 1 and 2; and *Report of the UN/ECA/FAO Economic Survey Mission on the Economic Development of Zambia* (the Seers Report), (Falcon Press, Ndola, 1964), Table VI-I.

3 THE DISTRIBUTION OF EMPLOYMENT AND INCOMES IN ZAMBIA

In Chapters 5, 6 and 7, on 'Issues in Wage Determination' and 'Prices and Incomes Policy', a great many of the leading issues concerning the distribution of income and employment within Zambia are analysed. These chapters examine in varying degrees of detail the origins of sectoral and skill-based earnings differentials. They also provide an understanding of the thrust of government policy regarding incomes, particularly in the modern sector, and help to explain the pattern of governmental relations with organised wage labour. Yet the discussion of these later chapters is largely dictated by the emphases of government labour policy, and thus reflects the disproportionate concentration of such policy upon features relating to wage employment in the modern sector.

The present chapter and Chapter 4, on 'The Distribution of Income' in Zambia, seek to present a more balanced picture of the entire labour market within Zambia, rural as well as urban, the traditional as well as the modern sector, against which other chapters should be viewed. Much of what follows will be descriptive, since a lot of ground has to be covered merely to understand the basic facts of the distribution of employment and income inside Zambia. However, it will be the contention of both chapters that a consistent underlying pattern of behaviour may be discerned in the events of the past 15 years.

Before 1964, the year of independence, the Zambian labour market was in a fundamental disequilibrium. The pre-independence colonial system of controls on population movement effectively restricted the flow of migrants to the main towns. With urban wage levels maintained well above rural incomes, the expected income available to an unskilled worker in the towns exceeded that available in rural areas. In normal circumstances, migration might have been expected to have occurred, away from the rural areas into the towns, to eliminate the gap between expected incomes; but within the framework of the *chitupa* system of labour passes, along the lines of the notorious South African pass book, the equilibrating flow of migrants was not allowed to develop freely.

With the lifting of migration controls after the attainment of self-government, the required equilibrating transfer of labour could take place. The unemployment and underemployment of unskilled workers in the towns increased, while the proportion employed in the urban informal sector rose steeply. Modern sector wages grew rapidly in the early years of independence, but the structure of urban employment shifted so strongly towards the informal sector that the expected urban income for an unskilled worker was brought down to a level comparable to that obtainable in the rural areas—after making due allowance for the differences in the cost of living between the town and the countryside.

The eventual equilibrium of the labour market was still distorted to some extent by political intervention in the free operation of market forces. For example, urban wage rates were pulled up unexpectedly sharply in the wake of the unification of local and expatriate pay scales[1] and the Zambianisation of skilled and semi-skilled posts; licensing and other restrictions limited the possibilities for self-employment in the informal sector; and urban interests were successful in turning the terms of trade against agricultural producers. Yet sufficiently many variables were left undetermined by political decisions for an equilibrium still to be reached, largely, it would appear, as a result of the growth of the informal sector.

In part, the growth of the informal sector was an inevitable consequence of the attainment of a rural/urban migration balance. The real possibility that a migrant would have to accept a poorly paid informal sector job acted as an effective equilibrating counterweight to the attraction of high formal sector wages. However, although equilibrium could well have occurred with the creation of a small number of very low-paid informal sector jobs, or, more in line with conventional wisdom, with the creation of a fair number of moderately well paid informal sector jobs alongside the growth of a pool of unemployment, Zambia avoided both the worst aspects of low income and high unemployment.

Instead, it appears that, while formal sector employment, created mainly by extra government spending, grew rapidly, the authorities did not provide full supporting facilities such as housing. Consequently these services were supplied by the informal sector. And, of course, once unofficial housing areas had been established to house formal sector workers, it was natural that the informal sector should expand to provide retail and repair services, fuel (like charcoal or firewood), and alcoholic beverages and entertainment, as well as simple manufactured goods. Contrary to expectations, the informal sector did not have to cut its prices (and incomes) substantially to grow through the substitution of its output for formal sector products. Rather, the structure of urban housing altered in such a way as to open up a large new market protected from formal sector competition.

The absorptive role of the urban informal sector is a theme to which we shall return. But to set our discussion in an appropriate context, we shall first examine the composition of the labour force that will be the subject of our subsequent analysis.

Population and Labour Force

Zambia is one of the most urbanised nations in Africa. Using a narrow definition of urban areas, considering only towns with a population of at least 5,000 within the township boundary, over one-third of the population lives in urban areas. Including smaller townships and peri-urban areas in the definition of urban areas would bring the urban population up to near one-half of the national total. The labour force statistics are similar. Of the potential adult labour force, around one-half live in urban and peri-urban areas, though, generally speaking, the urban proportions of the male labour force and of young adults are higher than the national average. Since the urban areas of Zambia tend to be concentrated along the main line of rail, the urban population will be found mainly in Copperbelt, Central and, to a lesser extent, Southern Provinces. The extent of the migration from other provinces towards these provinces, and of male and younger adults in particular, is revealed in Table 3.1, page 52, derived from data presented in the final report of the 1969 Population Census, and the provisional report of the 1974 sample census. The regional, sex and age-group differences in the distribution of the population and labour force are brought out more clearly when the data are presented as percentages of national totals, as is done in Table 3.2, page 53.

The rate of migration towards urban areas in the period 1963-9 was boosted by the once-and-for-all adjustment of the labour force away from the disequilibrium prevailing in 1963, and so it would be misleading to extrapolate from past trends to estimate future population movements. The preliminary results of the 1974 Sample Population Census show a decrease, from 8.9 to 6.8 per cent, in the annual population rate of growth in urban areas and an increase, from 0.5 to 1.2 per cent, in the rural population growth rate, but it is evident from Tables 3.1 and 3.2 that the younger active members of the labour force are already mainly in urban areas, and it can only be a matter of time before the general population is predominantly urbanised.

Despite the high proportion of the labour force recorded as living in urban areas, the number of workers employed in modern sector jobs is

Table 3.1: Distribution of Population by Province (Totals)

Province	Total population 1963	Total population 1969	1969 males between ages 15 and 60	1969 males* between ages 20 and 24	1969 females between ages 15 and 60	1969 females* between ages 20 and 24	Total population 1974
Central	505,000	713,000	192,300	30,100	175,400	34,500	920,000
Copperbelt	543,000	816,000	223,600	35,300	186,700	40,900	1,046,000
Eastern	480,000	510,000	102,800	13,100	145,800	24,000	568,000
Luapula	357,000	336,000	72,700	9,200	87,700	15,300	321,000
Northern	564,000	545,000	108,400	13,900	142,400	24,300	580,000
North Western	211,000	232,000	52,600	5,700	68,500	10,000	256,000
Southern	466,000	496,000	114,200	15,200	122,300	21,600	540,000
Western	362,000	410,000	91,900	9,700	124,200	18,900	463,000
Total for 3 line of rail provinces	1,514,000	2,025,000	530,100	80,600	484,400	97,000	2,506,000
Total for 5 rural provinces	1,976,000	2,032,000	428,400	51,700	568,600	92,400	2,189,000
National total	3,490,000	4,057,000	958,500	132,300	1,053,000	189,400	4,695,000

*Note the remarkable difference between the male and female totals in these two columns, a difference which also extends to the 25-29 age group. The only explanation can be women overstating their ages, assuming that there are no enumeration errors.

Table 3.2: Distribution of Population by Province (percentages)

Province	Total population 1963	Total population 1969	1969 males between ages 15 and 60	1969 males between ages 20 and 24	1969 females between ages 15 and 60	1969 females between ages 20 and 24	Total population 1974
Central	14.5	17.6	20.1	22.7	16.6	18.3	19.6
Copperbelt	15.6	20.1	23.3	26.6	17.7	21.6	22.2
Eastern	13.8	12.6	10.7	9.9	13.8	12.7	12.1
Luapula	10.3	8.3	7.6	6.9	8.3	8.1	6.8
Northern	16.2	13.4	11.3	10.5	13.5	12.8	12.4
North Western	6.1	5.7	5.5	4.3	6.5	5.3	5.5
Southern	13.4	12.2	11.9	11.5	11.6	11.4	11.5
Western	10.4	10.1	9.6	7.3	11.8	10.0	9.9
Total for 3 line of rail provinces	43.4	49.9	55.3	60.9	45.9	51.2	54.3
Total for 5 rural provinces	56.6	50.1	44.7	39.1	54.1	48.8	45.7
National total	100.0	100.0	100.0	100.0	100.0	100.0	100.0

low. Out of a labour force numbering nearly 2,000,000 in 1969, only 300,000 or so were modern sector wage earners. Around 150,000 were employed in the urban informal sector or as domestic servants, while as many as 120,000 relied upon paid employment in traditional agriculture for the bulk of their income; 650,000 were 'working proprietors' in traditional agriculture,[2] but the largest group of all, 800,000 strong, consisted of housewives, students, unemployed workers and people not seeking work.

Rural Employment

If we focus our attention upon the rural sector for a moment, we shall observe that a large proportion of the households there rely upon non-agricultural activities for the bulk of their monetary incomes. The 1970-1 Census of Agriculture reports that, of an estimated 632,400 farming households not involved in large-scale commercial agriculture in the rural areas of Zambia in 1970, only 293,800 produced a marketed or bartered surplus of agricultural produce during the year. The size distribution of agricultural holdings confirms that agriculture cannot provide the main source of income for many Zambian rural families.

Figure 3.1: Distribution of Land Holdings in Rural Areas by Size (Traditional Farmers Only)

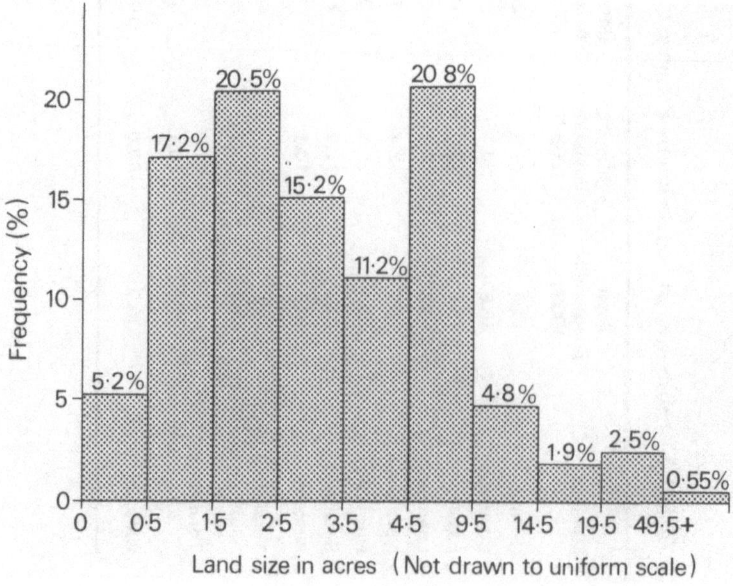

Source: *1970-1 Census of Agriculture* (First Report), Table 1.2.

From Figure 3.1, page 54, we note that around 43 per cent of rural households farm less than 2.5 acres of land, an acreage which, with Zambian land-extensive methods of cultivation, can scarcely be sufficient to meet even a household's own food requirements. For these households, cash incomes must have come mainly from non-agricultural activities. In this context, it is worth mentioning a labour force study of Luapula Province that the author undertook in late 1975. This estimated the number of formal sector employees in the province at 8,000, the number of informal sector workers also at 8,000, and the number of fishermen at 15,000-20,000. Therefore, one might reasonably suppose that up to one half of the province's households depended upon pensions or remittances from the line of rail for the bulk of their cash incomes.

Table 3.3: Provincial Distribution of Holdings by Size

	Size of agricultural holdings in rural areas			
Province	Number of holdings	% under 2.5 acres	% 2.5-9.5 acres	% over 9.5 acres
Central	72,600	33.0	49.7	17.3
Copperbelt	17,300	47.8	47.8	4.4
Eastern	121,300	39.3	55.4	5.3
Luapula	81,000	68.0	31.1	0.9
Northern	120,100	50.9	46.6	3.5
North Western	53,000	47.4	49.4	3.2
Southern	78,500	24.5	39.0	36.5
Western	88,800	36.5	55.7	7.8
National total	632,600	42.9	47.2	9.8

Analysed on a provincial basis, the distribution of agricultural holdings by size shows Southern, Central and, to a lesser extent, Western and Eastern Provinces to be the main centres for Zambian emergent farmers. As Table 3.3, above, indicates, the four remaining provinces, in which *chitemene* methods of cultivation are practised, tend to have the smallest agricultural plots (though it should be remembered that Luapula and Northern Provinces would be expected to have smaller plots since fishing provides a major source of income in those provinces).

Urban Employment

For information on urban employment, we shall also rely heavily upon census data, although, since the methods of social surveys and census tabulation make it extremely difficult to collect data on all urban areas as a group, most of the evidence presented in the following discussion is drawn from one urban district, Lusaka Urban. Comparative census statistics on the employment of the male labour force in Lusaka in 1963 and 1969 are given in Table 3.4, below.

Table 3.4: Distribution of Male Labour Force in Lusaka (using 1973 City Boundaries)

% of labour force	1963 Census (%)	1969 Census (%)
(a) Self-employed and unpaid family workers	6.1	10.6
(b) Wage employees	83.2	75.5
(c) Unemployed	10.7	13.9

*Note that in 1963 many unpaid family workers were classified either as unemployed or as people not actively involved in the labour force.

As it stands, Table 3.4 indicates that between 1963 and 1969 a steady growth occurred in unemployment and non-wage employment, at the expense of wage employment. This is in line with the suggestion made at the start of this chapter, that equilibrium in the labour market was attained through the expansion of low-income alternatives to wage employment in the towns. However, the interpretations to be put on the concepts of unemployment, unpaid family workers, and labour force participation are highly uncertain, particularly where the adult female population is concerned. This is brought out by Table 3.5, page 57, which gives the census breakdown of the labour force characteristics of Lusaka Urban district in 1969.

Unfortunately, the Census, by virtue of its lack of depth and variable quality of responses, may not be a reliable source of information. More useful and reliable are systematic studies of selected townships in the main urban areas. A number of these are summarised in Table 3.6, page 58, which gives labour force characteristics for heads of households where possible. Since household heads are usually households' breadwinners, it can be argued that it is their employment behaviour which is one of the greatest importance in a study like the present one.

On the basis of Table 3.6, it would appear that the census figures

Table 3.5: 1969 Labour Force Characteristics in Lusaka

	Males (% of labour force)		Females (% of labour force)		Total (% of labour force)	
Number over 15 years of age	77,372		62,420		139,792	
Labour force	67,292	(100.0%)	18,989	(100.0%)	86,281	(100.0%)
Unemployed	9,375	(13.9%)	9,762	(51.4%)	19,137	(22.2%)
Working	57,917	(86.1%)	9,227	(48.6%)	67,144	(77.8%)
of which:						
Wage employed	50,783	(75.5%)	5,351	(28.2%)	56,134	(65.1%)
Self-employed and employers	4,717	(7.0%)	935	(4.9%)	5,652	(6.6%)
Unpaid family workers	2,417	(3.6%)	2,941	(15.5%)	5,358	(6.2%)

give a misleadingly high impression of the problem of unemployment and understate the amount of non-wage employment. Bearing in mind the higher level of unemployment and non-wage employment in informal than in formal housing areas, Table 3.6 suggests that among all Lusaka household heads the unemployment rate may be only 5 per cent, with 15 per cent of the total labour force in non-wage employment. This leaves the important question of the breakdown of wage employment between the formal and informal sectors still to be discussed, and we shall turn to this very shortly. Before doing so, it is worth emphasising one of the implications of the analysis just presented, which is that the problem of pure unemployment is less serious than is often supposed. Furthermore, those who are unemployed in Zambia tend to be young, fairly well qualified, and financially able to afford to remain unemployed for lengthy periods. A project tracing the careers of secondary school leavers, for example, found that up to one-third of them were unemployed six months after leaving school in 1971, despite their excellent employment prospects. The Chawama study mentioned in Table 3.6 provides further evidence for this optimistic view of unemployment. The details of the ages of the Chawama unemployed, given in Table 3.7, page 59, show that a person under 25 years of age is five times as likely to be unemployed as an older worker.

If our view is correct, the main problem to be overcome as regards

Table 3.6: Labour Force Characteristics in Selected Townships

Township	Type of settlement	Year of survey	Coverage of survey	Percentage distribution of labour force surveyed: Unemployed (%)	Employees (%)	Employers, unpaid family workers and self-employed (%)
Zambia City (Luanshya)	Informal peri-urban	1966	Household heads	4	32	64
New Kanyama (Lusaka)	Informal site and service	1966	Lodgers	4	←96→	
New Kanyama (Lusaka)	Informal site and service	1969	Males (Census)	12	79	9
Nguluwe (Lusaka)	Informal	1967	Household heads	5	89	6
Kalingalinga (Lusaka)	Informal	1967	Household heads	6	77	17
Kalingalinga (Lusaka)	Informal	1969	Males (Census)	12	75	14
Matero (Lusaka)	Council housing	1969	Males (Census)	15	74	11
Woodlands (Lusaka)	High income	1969	Males (Census)	7	91	2
George/ Mwaziona (Lusaka)	Informal	1969	Males (Census)	12	76	12
George/ Mwaziona (Lusaka)	Informal	1973	Household heads	7	77	16
Chawama (Lusaka)	Informal	1974	Labour force	9	68	23

Sources: Besides the 1969 Population Census, the main sources for this table are, Zambia City, New Kanyama (1966), Nguluwe (1967) and Kalingalinga (1967), the various Department of Community Development Reports; for Mwaziona (1973), Department of Town and Country Planning; and for Chawama, the Development Planning Unit, University College, London.

Table 3.7: The Unemployed in Chawama (Lusaka) in 1974

	Male		Female		Unemployed
	Working	Unemployed	Working	Unemployed	as % of total
Under 25 years old	83	24	24	7	22.5
Over 25 years old	401	20	51	3	4.8
Total	484	44	75	10	8.8

Table 3.8: Informal Sector Employment, by Economic Activity (percentages)

<table>
<tr><th></th><th>Mwaziona (%)</th><th>Chawama (%)</th></tr>
<tr><td>Large-scale retail (including bars)</td><td>11</td><td>16</td></tr>
<tr><td>Market type retail</td><td rowspan="2">43</td><td>28</td></tr>
<tr><td>Small retail</td><td>15</td></tr>
<tr><td>Building sector</td><td>12</td><td>2</td></tr>
<tr><td>Manufacturing</td><td>6</td><td>11</td></tr>
<tr><td>Repair</td><td>5</td><td>8</td></tr>
<tr><td>Fuel distribution</td><td>20</td><td>12</td></tr>
<tr><td>Landlords</td><td>2</td><td>3</td></tr>
<tr><td>Others</td><td>2</td><td>4</td></tr>
</table>

Table 3.9: Employment Distribution in Lusaka, 1969 (in thousands)

Formal sector employment	50			
Domestic servants	10			
Self-employed informal sector workers	6		Fuel distribution	2.5
Wage employed informal sector workers	6	of whom	Retail workers	10
Unpaid family informal sector workers	6		Construction	2
Unemployed (of whom many take casual work)	8		Manufacturing and repair	2.5
			Other	1

Zambia's urban labour force is the expansion of income-earning opportunities in the informal sector rather than an elimination of unemployment. It is to an analysis of these opportunities that we now turn.

Urban Informal Sector Employment

Since Lusaka data are more readily available than data for other towns, in this section I shall mainly summarise the conclusions that I derived from a study of employment characteristics in Lusaka, carried out for the University College, London, Development Planning Unit's 1973-5 survey of absorption in Lusaka. Later one can try to extend the results derived for Lusaka to other urban areas of Zambia.

Urban informal sector employment can usefully be divided into two distinct categories: domestic service, which really lies somewhere between modern sector and informal sector wage employment; and small-scale production and service activities. To take domestic servants first, Bettinson's 1957 survey of Lusaka carried out for the Rhodes-Livingstone Institute estimated that at that time there were approximately 5,000 domestic servants' households in the capital city. Between 1957 and 1969 the number of high-income households in Lusaka doubled, while the total number of households more than trebled. In the circumstances, to extrapolate from Bettinson's figures and suppose that there were at least 10,000 domestic servants' households in Lusaka in 1969 seems conservative.

The figure of at least 10,000 domestic servants in Lusaka in 1969 is supported by the University College Development Planning Unit's estimate that, in 1973, 8,000 households in high-cost housing areas were providing services for high-income recipients. Allowing for population growth since 1969 would mean that 6,000 or more domestic servants were living in high-cost areas of Lusaka in 1969. In addition, the surveys of low-cost townships mentioned in Table 3.6 indicate that an average of over 6 per cent of the labour force in them works as domestic servants. This would add 4,000-5,000 domestic servants to the 6,000 living in high-cost areas in 1969. Accordingly, we shall assume that 10,000-11,000 people worked as domestic servants in Lusaka in 1969, which compares with the 1969 Census figure of 6,321 adult males classified as domestic servants.

The estimation of employment in other urban informal sector activities depends crucially upon one's beliefs about the division of the informal sector labour force between employers and self-employed, unpaid family workers and paid employees. The 1969 Population Census fails to distinguish between formal and informal wage employment, but, as Table 3.5 reveals, derives very similar estimates for the number who were self-employed/employers and the number who were unpaid family workers. The 1974 Chawama survey records virtually identical numbers of unpaid family workers and informal sector wage employees in its findings. Both the census and Chawama results are broadly consistent with the general conclusions of Oberschall's work on traders in George compound, Lusaka,[3] and of Nat Tembo's surveys of Luburma and Chawama markets for the University College, London team, which suggest that employment in the informal sector may be divided 1 : 1 : 1 as between employers or self-employed/wage employees/unpaid family workers. In small trading enterprises the ratio is nearer to 1 : 0 : 1; in larger-scale trading the ratio will be 1 : 1 : 1; and in stores, bars, construction firms, manufacturing and repair enterprises, it may be 1 : 2 : 1. With the 1969 Census figures as a guide, we might reasonably expect to find 6,000 self-employed workers and employers, 6,000 wage employees and 6,000 unpaid family workers in Lusaka's informal sector in 1969.

Both the 1974 Chawama survey and the 1973 Mwaziona survey provide details of the occupations of the informal sector workers in their samples. Their results are summarised in Table 3.8, page 59, in which it should be remembered that, since the Mwaziona survey covered only heads of households, it will understate the numbers employed in the large-scale retail sector, in the building trade, in manufacturing and in repair services, and will overstate other areas of employment. The Chawama results correspond closely to those from Mwaziona, with the sole exception of the construction employment totals, which were exceptionally reduced by the fact that the Chawama survey was undertaken during the slack (rainy) construction season. The details of expenditures on building labour in both Chawama and Mwaziona are compatible with the informal construction sector accounting for 12-15 per cent of total informal sector employment, equivalent to 2,000-2,500 workers; and this is in line with the discrepancy between the 1969 Census total of (formal and informal) construction sector employment in Lusaka (7,056) and the Central Statistical Office's 1972 figures of formal construction sector employment for companies based in Lusaka (5,278).

Pulling all these strands together, one arrives at the tentative distribution of employment in Lusaka in 1969 shown in Table 3.9, page 59. If the Lusaka statistics accurately reflect the distribution of employment in other urban areas of Zambia, then Table

3.10, below, represents an estimate of the national urban employment position.

Table 3.10: National Breakdown of Urban Employment, 1969 (in thousands)

Formal sector employment	300			
Domestic servants	60			
Self-employed informal sector workers	40		Fuel distribution	15
			Retail sector	60
Wage employed informal sector workers	35	of whom	Construction	12
Unpaid family informal sector workers	35		Manufacturing and repair	15
Unemployed	45		Other	8

Urban Formal Sector Employment

Much of the discussion of urban informal sector employment has had to be speculative, in view of the absence of any comprehensive statistics on the topic. Yet it is evident that the informal sector constitutes an important, and an increasingly important, portion of the urban labour market. The position of the formal, modern wage employment sector is much better documented, and more widely acknowledged as an instrument for labour absorption in Zambia. In Tables 3.11 and 3.12, pages 63 and 64, we summarise the Central Statistical Office's (CSO's) statistics on formal sector employment, which include details of agricultural employment, and thus extend slightly beyond a purely urban frame of reference. In December 1972, the CSO changed over from a racial African/ Non-African listing of employment to a nationally-based Zambian/ Non-Zambian one, and accordingly Tables 3.11 and 3.12 do likewise.

From Tables 3.11 and 3.12 we observe how strongly the economy responded to the rapid growth in public sector expenditure after independence with the recurrent expenditure up from K111.6 million in the 1964/5 financial year to a budgeted K633.1 million in 1977, and capital expenditure up from K30.6 million to K159.4 million over the same period. Public sector expenditure, financed out of a growing proportion of rising copper mining profits until 1974, was undoubtedly the prime motive force behind

Table 3.11: African Formal Sector Employment, 1960-76*

			Sector				of which		
Year	Agriculture	Mining	Manufacturing	Construction	Other	Total	Public sector		Private sector
1960	37,000	42,700	17,900	36,000	65,400	209,000	–		–
1963	36,000	40,800	15,900	23,400	73,900	190,000	–		–
1964	34,500	42,500	18,000	29,100	77,400	201,500	–		–
1965	31,020	44,730	24,730	44,740	87,540	232,760	–		–
1966	31,540	46,570	27,180	58,310	85,880	249,480	84,470		165,010
1967	36,060	48,480	28,500	60,580	101,030	274,650	102,710		171,940
1968	36,280	49,150	31,390	67,420	106,560	290,800	108,820		181,980
1969	37,520	49,420	32,730	57,470	114,490	291,630	116,890		174,740
1970	33,480	51,060	33,920	66,740	125,120	310,320	126,990		183,330
1971	37,270	52,380	37,660	67,470	136,900	331,680	136,490		195,190
1972	37,690	52,090	39,840	66,220	142,910	338,750	138,580		200,170
				Zambian employment					
1973	30,330	50,420	40,460	66,630	152,210	340,050	141,630		198,420
1974	32,160	54,270	40,970	66,270	157,920	351,590	146,710		204,880
							Public sector	Parastatal sector	Private sector
1975	34,960	56,510	41,680	69,220	162,960	365,330	121,690	120,150	123,490
1976	32,530	53,500	39,780	51,340+	158,710	335,860	121,030	112,880	101,950+

*Note that the figures until 1964 are yearly averages. Thereafter, with the exception of 1973 and 1974 (which refer to the December quarter) they refer to the June quarter. The same convention is adopted in Table 3.12.

+Excluding Tan Zam railway employment. However, the construction of the railway was virtually complete in early 1976; hence the inclusion of such employment would make a negligible difference to the total in the construction sector.

Table 3.12: Non-African Formal Sector Employment, 1960-76

Year	Sector Mining	Total	of which Public sector		Private sector
1960	8.030	33,000	–		–
1963	8,230	32,500	–		–
1964	8,290	31,700	–		–
1965	6,560	33,840	–		–
1966	7,490	28,880	7,800		21,080
1967	6,630	29,080	7,970		21,400
1968	5,780	28,930	7,980		20,960
1969	5,970	29,820	8,920		20,900
1970	5,450	27,430	7,760		19,670
1971	5,600	26,680	6,480		20,200
1972	5,430	25,990	7,270		18,720
		Non-Zambian employment			
1973	11,320	33,390	7,630		25,760
1974	10,840	33,300	7,540		25,760
			Public sector	Parastatal sector	Private sector
1975	10,250	33,510	6,580	13,000	13,930
1976	12,380	32,500	6,820	14,810	10,870

the growth in formal sector employment before 1976, but one must not overlook the contribution of the growth in the manufacturing sector in the wake of Rhodesia's unilateral declaration of independence (UDI). Protected from Rhodesian competition, import-substitution industries flourished during the first decade of Zambian political independence; but their growth has scarcely been sufficient to offset the effects of cutbacks in real government expenditure, such as occurred in 1969, between 1971 and 1973, and, most savagely, after 1975.

Regional Formal Sector Employment

Despite the growing importance of the public sector in overall wage employment, and a relative bias (in comparison with the private sector) of the public sector towards employment creation in the less developed provinces of Zambia, these provinces have gained little from the growth in national formal sector employment. All provinces managed to increase their absolute levels of wage employment between 1963 and 1975, but

Table 3.13: Regional Formal Sector African Employment, 1963-75

Province	Population (000)		Formal sector wage employment			Of 1968 employment	
	1963	1974	1963*	1968	1975+	Public sector	Private sector
Central (including Lusaka)	505	920	56,590	92,930	114,260	38,680	53,980
Copperbelt	544	1,046	119,720	140,420	149,910	24,620	116,430
Eastern	480	568	11,940	12,860	13,120	9,740	3,980
Luapula	357	321	6,250	7,400	7,650	5,480	1,690
Northern	564	580	9,300	12,860	24,640	11,260	2,140
North Western	211	256	5,970	6,860	5,990	5,030	1,310
Southern	466	540	34,750	36,380	38,140	16,920	18,230
Western	363	463	8,770	10,030	11,620	8,100	1,020
Total	3,490	4,695	256,290	318,610	365,330	119,830	198,780

*The 1963 figure includes 35,000 domestic servants.

+The 1975 statistics are for 'Zambians', not 'Africans'. This has the effect of reducing the 1975 Copperbelt figure by 7,000 and the Eastern Province figure by 400.

the absolute increases in Central and Copperbelt Provinces exceed those in the other six provinces combined. The most important shift to have occurred over this period has been towards wage employment creation in Central Province rather than on the Copperbelt. A summary of the regional employment statistics is given in Table 3.13, page 65.

The upsurge in Northern Province employment between 1968 and 1975 is almost entirely a result of the construction work on the Tan Zam railway, and one must expect that employment in the province will have fallen back somewhat after 1975. Unfortunately, the medium-term outlook for employment creation in the rural provinces is not encouraging. The Second National Development Plan (SNDP), covering the 1972-76 period, marked a move away from the infrastructural emphasis of the First Plan towards more immediately productive investments, which, by their nature, tend to be biased in favour of large urban centres. The impact of the new stress on development strategy extends beyond the regional distribution of wage employment since the strategy also affects the overall level of employment creation and, in this respect, too, the new strategy marks an unfortunate change in direction.

Elsewhere,[4] the author has estimated the employment and import-generating direct and indirect effects of expanding sectoral outputs. Using standard input-output techniques, one derives the results summarised in Table 3.14, page 67. A ranking of planned sectoral growth rates during the SNDP (manufacturing 14.7 per cent; distribution and tourism 8.9 per cent; construction 8.1 per cent; transport and communications 7.2 per cent; mining 6.1 per cent; agriculture 5.9 per cent; and services 5.6 per cent) runs in almost reverse order to a ranking of these sectors on the basis of Table 3.14, if one gives a positive weight to the creation of local employment and a negative weight to the expansion of imports and the employment of expatriate workers. If the sectoral forecasts of the SNDP are carried forward to the Third National Development Plan, the prognosis for wage employment creation is not good. Yet, even before the presentation of the SNDP, the rate of growth of formal sector employment had been slowing down from the levels of the mid-1960s.

There are several hypotheses that might be advanced to explain the slower growth of formal sector employment. The structure of the economy might have been shifting towards sectors that are relatively capital intensive. This is unlikely, given the rapid growth of the service sectors, which Table 3.14 shows to be unusually labour intensive. The share of national income being reinvested to provide for future growth in output and employment might have fallen. However, gross investment as a share

Table 3.14: Imports Generated and Employment Created by Increased Demand for Products*

Sector	Imports generated (in Kwacha) for a K1,000 increase in final demand for this sector's products	Non-African employment created by a K1,000 increase in final demand for this sector's products	African employment created by a K1,000 increase in final demand for this sector's products
Forestry and commercial farming	756.9 (4)	0.03449 (23)	1.266 (3)
Fishing	557.8 (16)	0.04065 (17)	7.513 (1)
Metal mining	244.5 (40)	0.02450 (32)	0.2035 (36)
Other mining	504.3 (22)	0.03351 (25)	0.7831 (10)
Meat processing	840.2 (2)	0.04336 (24)	0.6233 (16)
Dairies	654.2 (8)	0.04439 (15)	0.9104 (7)
Grain mills	672.6 (7)	0.03451 (22)	0.6759 (13)
Bakeries	555.0 (17)	0.03862 (19)	0.5363 (17)
Other food	731.9 (5)	0.01689 (40)	0.1976 (37)
Breweries and tobacco	339.5 (37)	0.01879 (39)	0.1806 (29)
Textiles and clothing	624.2 (10)	0.02465 (31)	0.4348 (19)
Wood products	578.9 (13)	0.03761 (21)	0.5742 (16)
Paper products	928.6 (1)	0.1083 (2)	0.7093 (12)
Rubber products	461.0 (29)	0.03101 (28)	0.2977 (30)
Chemicals	636.7 (9)	0.02288 (35)	0.2493 (22)
Clay products	489.3 (23)	0.02778 (30)	1.046 (4)
Cement	423.3 (35)	0.03202 (26)	0.3917 (21)
Foundries	578.5 (14)	0.03862 (19)	0.3088 (29)
Machinery	607.8 (11)	0.02183 (37)	0.2066 (34)
Electrical equipment	484.6 (26)	0.06203 (9)	0.3636 (26)
Transport equipment	535.0 (20)	0.02444 (33)	0.2054 (35)
Other manufactures	582.8 (12)	0.05222 (12)	0.3472 (28)
Construction	516.0 (21)	0.04199 (16)	0.7559 (11)
Electricity and water	681.2 (6)	0.02218 (36)	0.1848 (38)
Distribution	423.6 (34)	0.05445 (10)	0.3829 (22)
Banks and insurance	281.4 (39)	0.08637 (5)	0.2161 (33)
Real estate	298.1 (38)	0.02428 (34)	0.2658 (31)
Railway transport	466.8 (28)	0.04912 (13)	0.3804 (24)
Road transport	453.6 (31)	0.04032 (18)	0.4549 (18)
Other transport	484.9 (25)	0.08884 (4)	0.4152 (20)
Posts and telecommunications	554.6 (18)	0.03193 (27)	0.3495 (27)
Government administration	456.2 (30)	0.06620 (8)	0.8182 (8)

Sector	Imports generated (in Kwacha) for a K1,000 increase in final demand for this sector's products	Non-African employment created by a K1,000 increase in final demand for this sector's products	African employment created by a K1,000 increase in final demand for this sector's products
Education	436.0 (32)	0.1397 (1)	0.9661 (6)
Health	483.4 (27)	0.06663 (7)	0.6032 (15)
Business services	378.8 (36)	0.07535 (6)	0.3746 (25)
Non-business services	541.5 (19)	0.1070 (3)	1.024 (5)
Hotels and restaurants	424.0 (33)	0.05276 (11)	0.8097 (9)
Other personal services	489.0 (24)	0.04491 (14)	3.377 (2)
Unspecified	775.3 (3)	0.01982 (38)	0.1788 (40)
Private consumption	574.4 (15)	0.03085 (29)	0.3828 (23)

*The figures in brackets denote the rank of a sector in that column.
Source: J. Fry and C.R.M. Harvey, 'Copper and Zambia', in J. Cownie and S. Pearson (eds.), *Commodity Exports and African Economic Development* (Lexington Books, Boston, 1974).

of Gross Domestic Product rose steadily from 11.4 per cent in 1964 to 32.5 per cent in 1968, and was still 28.4 per cent in 1976, albeit out of a depressed level of GDP. Technology might have been pushing all sectors of the economy in an increasingly capital-intensive, less labour-intensive, direction. Or, the most popular explanation, high and rising labour costs were encouraging the substitution of capital for labour. Jacob Mwanza[5] has tested this hypothesis, using a CES production function, over the period 1955-66 in the Zambian mining and manufacturing sectors. Where Q = real sectoral value added, E = sectoral wage employment, W = average real earnings, b_1 = the elasticity of substitution, and b_2 measures the returns to scale ($b_2 = 0$ for constant returns to scale, and is strictly positive for strictly increasing returns to scale), one can derive an equation of the form:

$$e = a - b_1 w + (1 - b_2)q$$

where a = constant, and e, w and q measure proportional rates of growth, i.e.

$$q = \frac{dQ/dt}{Q}$$

The regression result for the manufacturing sector was:

$$e = 0.51 - \underset{(0.35)}{0.62w} + \underset{(0.13)}{0.55q} \qquad (R^2 = 0.698) \ldots\ldots\ldots\ldots\ldots (1)$$

and for the mining sector was:

$$e = 0.24 - \underset{(0.31)}{0.55w} + \underset{(0.18)}{0.66q} \qquad (R^2 = 0.44) \ldots\ldots\ldots\ldots\ldots (2)$$

At the 10 per cent significance level, therefore, one would accept that the elasticity of substitution in Zambia's mining and manufacturing sectors was strictly positive. In other words, higher wages relative to the costs of capital reduce the labour/capital ratio. In terms of both equations (1) and (2), this implies also that a higher rate of growth of wages leads to a lower rate of growth of employment.

Mwanza's regressions cover data only for the period between 1955 and 1966. After 1966 wage employment grew at an even slower rate. Equations (1) and (2) suggest that this may have been due in part to the deceleration in the growth of output after 1966 which took place in both the mining and manufacturing sectors; but it may also have been caused by an acceleration in the rate of increase of wages after 1965. In the next chapter, on the distribution of income, evidence will be presented to show that such an acceleration did occur.

Notes

1. This is discussed fully in Chapter 5.
2. These figures for employment in agriculture are drawn from the first report of the *1970-1 Census of Agriculture.*
3. Described in part in 'African Businessmen and Small Traders in Lusaka', *African Social Research*, 16 (1973).
4. In J. Fry and C.R.M. Harvey, 'Copper and Zambia', in J. Cownie and S. Pearson (eds), *Commodity Exports and African Economic Development* (Lexington Books, Boston, 1974).
5. In 'Modern Sector Employment Growth in East Africa (with special emphasis on Zambia)', (unpublished PhD thesis, Cornell University, Ithaca, 1973), Ch. V.

4 THE DISTRIBUTION OF INCOME

Rural Incomes

As in the case of employment, statistics on incomes in the rural areas of Zambia tend to be few and far between, and provide only a patchy coverage of one or two favoured districts.

The Central Statistical Office (CSO) publishes an estimate of 'Rural Household Consumption of its Own Products' in the National Accounts, although its figures are allegedly based upon a pre-Second World War rural budget survey in one rural district. These figures are given in Table 4.1, page 71, where GDP is broken down into the main categories of income. On the basis of these estimates, the imputed value of the consumption by a typical rural household of its own production was approximately K240 per annum in 1976. In 1969 prices, this was equivalent to an income of K130 per annum. While this tallies well with some recent surveys of rural incomes, there are serious differences with others. To bring out the nature of these differences, a summary of the three most important recent estimates of rural incomes will be useful.

The first, and undoubtedly the most detailed, was the UNZALPI survey.[1] The UNZALPI survey consisted of a study of 239 small-scale farmers in two widely separated rural districts: Mumbwa in Central Province and Katete in Eastern Province. After having observed the farmers' daily activities, consumption patterns and cash earnings over a period of years, the UNZALPI team divided farmers into 'villagers' and 'farmers'.

> Essentially [the distinction between them] is one of *motivation* . . . Villagers have no real interest in making a cash income out of farming . . . By contrast, farmers endeavour to produce a surplus to generate income . . . It is emphasized that the distinction between villagers and farmers is based on *intention* rather than achievement.[2]

This division is extremely controversial, but in as much as the differentiation corresponds to one between semi-commercial (more than 50 per cent of income from cash sales) and subsistence (less than 50 per cent of income from cash sales) farmers, then the UNZALPI results can be used to estimate subsistence incomes.

Valuing all food consumption at local market prices, the average

Table 4.1: GDP at Factor Cost, 1965-1976 (in K million)*

Year	Wages and salaries	Gross profits	Rural household consumption of own products	GDP at factor cost
1965	243.5	285.6	79.1	608.2
1966	281.6	343.5	84.5	709.6
1967	348.2	379.6	87.4	815.2
1968	386.1	388.5	92.4	867.0
1969	394.7	557.5	95.0	1,047.2
1970	482.7	516.8	94.6	1,094.1
1971	569.7	440.6	101.3	1,111.6
1972	636.5	489.0	105.5	1,231.0
1973	672.2	584.8	119.2	1,376.2
(1974)	778.0	694.0	132.0	1,604.0
(1975)	855.0	491.0	142.0	1,488.0
(1976)	940.0	522.0	166.0	1,628.0

*NB Figures for years in parentheses are provisional estimates.

annual incomes of 'farmers' in Mumbwa and Katete were K669 and K285 respectively. The corresponding annual incomes of 'villagers' were K230 and K125. If one were to add the imputed value of housing, water supplies and other household services to these figures and deduct cash incomes, then the CSO's estimates of subsistence incomes look quite reasonable.

The West German Report on Southern Province prepared for the Second National Development Plan[3] tends to support the UNZALPI results. Its sample of farmers earning less than K50 per annum from cash sales showed an average of only K90 of imputed annual household income derived from agriculture (though they received K141 from non-farm activities).

The only estimate of rural incomes based upon a nationwide sample, was that prepared for the Planning Office in 1970.[4] Despite having only a minority of its sample involved in commercial agriculture, the report estimates the 1969 income of a rural household at K360 per annum. Deducting cash incomes from this figure, the estimate of subsistence production and consumption is around K250 at 1969 prices. In 1976 prices, therefore, subsistence production would be worth K400-K450 per household per annum, according to the Planning Office's calculations.

Clearly there is a sizable discrepancy between the Planning Office estimate and the other three estimates of subsistence incomes. However, upon closer examination, the discrepancy can be seen to be attributable in part to the method of valuation of household services, such as housing. But the discrepancy can also be traced to the prices used to value agricultural output. The Planning Office 1969 estimate of an annual income of K250 from subsistence agriculture not only imputes a higher value of household services than other estimates (putting it at 38 per cent of agricultural earnings), but it is also the only estimate which values foodstuffs at urban retail prices rather than at the much lower rural marketing prices. Taking these two factors into account, all the estimates of subsistence incomes are quite closely in accord. Valued at 1969 rural prices, subsistence incomes are in the region of K130 per annum; valued at urban retail prices, they average K250 per annum.

While these estimates of subsistence incomes can be reconciled with one another to derive an acceptable valuation of subsistence incomes, they do little to inform us about the distribution of cash incomes of peasant farmers. For that purpose, the evidence in Figure 3.1, page 54, is probably the most useful that is available, since we may assume that the 54 per cent of all traditional farming households who do not produce a marketed or bartered surplus of agricultural produce correspond roughly to the 54 per cent of farming households with the smallest acreages under cultivation. Accordingly we may suppose that farmers with holdings exceeding 3.5 acres are regular producers of marketed surpluses of agricultural produce.

In Figure 4.1, page 73, we illustrate the implications of assuming that all land in excess of 3.5 acres is used to produce cash crops, and that each acre of cash crops produces the equivalent of 5 bags of maize, worth roughly K25. Alongside this representation of the frequency distribution of income from cash sales of agricultural produce and from subsistence activities, we present the results of the CSO's 1972/3 pilot rural budget survey, in which the total incomes (agricultural as well as non-agricultural, and from subsistence as well as cash production) of a small number (103) of rural households were tabulated.

Both distributions have a considerable margin of error, and Figure 4.1 must therefore be treated with caution. However, the distributions display the right-skewness that would be expected of them; and in the case of the 1970/1 survey, the income distribution that is derived is encouragingly consistent with the results of a survey of peasant farmers in the Pemba District of Southern Province carried out by Fabian Maimbo in 1972/3. This found that 55 per cent of the sample earned cash incomes in excess of K300 per annum, from the sale of agricultural

Figure 4.1: Distribution of Incomes in the Rural Sector

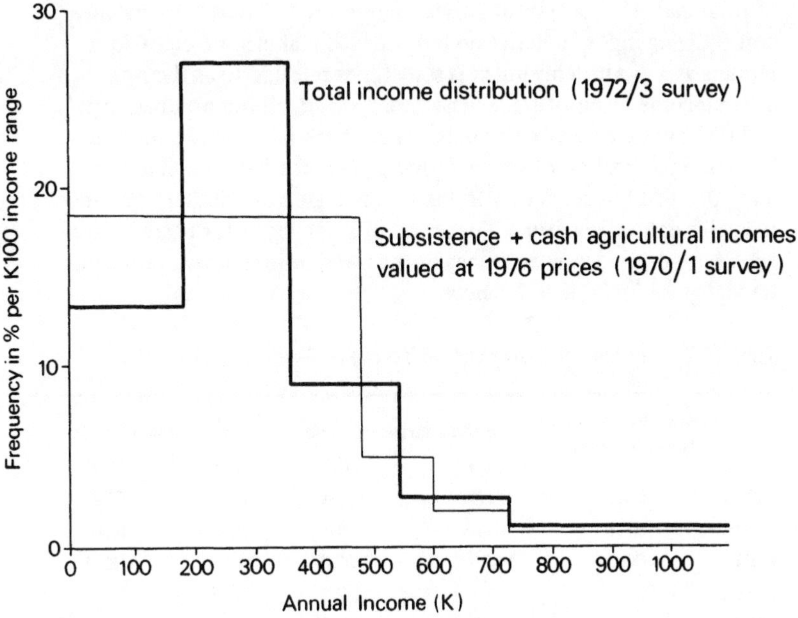

produce, and 6 per cent earned over K1,000 per annum. These figures are both about five times as large as one would expect on the basis of the 1970/1 survey, but, given the much greater than average development of traditional agriculture in Southern Province revealed in Table 3.3, page 55,[5] and the prominent position of the Pemba District in Southern Province agriculture, Maimbo's findings seem to support the general validity of Figure 4.1.

Rural-Urban Terms of Trade

Useful though our estimates of subsistence and peasant incomes are at a point in time, it is very difficult to derive from them measures of the change in real living standards over time. Accordingly, in 1971, Maimbo and the author investigated the changes that were occurring in the terms of trade facing African peasant farmers.[6] The estimates were based upon Laspeyre chain indices of the total volume of produce marketed by

African peasant farmers, where the produce was priced at prevailing producer prices. We also used the results of a preliminary budget survey of Southern Province peasant farmers, from which cost of living indices could be constructed relating only to cash purchases. The money value of total marketed output of African farmers was deflated by our own cost of living index to derive an index of the real income of African farmers as a group. This index is sometimes referred to as the rural-urban income terms of trade. The index of agricultural producer prices deflated by the cost of living index yielded the barter terms of trade. Since the publication of the 1971 paper, Maimbo has completed his more detailed budget survey in the Pemba region of Southern Province. Using his data to construct a new cost of living index for peasant farmers, I have derived new estimates of the trend in rural-urban terms of trade,[7] given in Table 4.2, below.

Table 4.2: Indices of Rural-Urban Terms of Trade (1964=100.0)

Year	Cost of living index for rural areas	Income terms of trade		Barter terms of trade	
		(a)*	(b)+	(a)*	(b)+
1960	97.0	NA	NA	NA	97.4
1963	97.3	NA	NA	NA	NA
1964	100.0	100.0	100.0	100.0	100.0
1965	105.2	91.1	92.1	95.7	96.0
1966	113.1	79.2	80.3	90.0	91.3
1967	117.5	121.6	130.7	93.1	85.2
1968	129.8	136.2	141.0	82.1	74.8
1969	133.0	109.8	114.9	79.0	71.6
1970	138.0	107.9	110.7	90.2	85.8
1971	146.3	171.5	204.1	86.7	83.0
1972	155.8	203.3	250.0	85.6	82.6
1973	166.1	NA	NA	81.3	78.6

* (a) refers to the case where agricultural production is taken to include fishing.
\+ (b) refers to the case where agricultural production is taken to exclude fishing.

The data presented in Table 4.2 paint a sorry picture of the impact upon African peasant agriculture of government agricultural producer pricing policy since 1964. All the most important commodities produced by peasant farmers, such as maize, cattle, tobacco, groundnuts, cotton or fish, are subject to government intervention in pricing policy. This intervention has almost certainly resulted in a fall in the real cash receipts of a peasant farmer between 1964 and 1972. Since the barter terms of trade measure the purchasing power of a representative *fixed* quantity of African peasant farmers' agricultural produce in terms of units of goods bought from the urban sector, we can observe from Table 4.2 that the real purchasing power of a unit of marketed peasant output has fallen by roughly 20 per cent between 1964 and 1973. However, against this must be noted the fact that the real purchasing power of *all* peasant cash income (the income terms of trade) more than doubled between 1964 and 1972. With a trebling of output between 1964 and 1972, peasant farmers, as a group, have become twice as well off.

One requires further information concerning the proportion of the increase in the column of marketed produce which came from farmers who entered semi-commercial farming for the first time between 1964 and 1972, before one can estimate how the cash income of a typical semi-commercial farmer will have changed over the period. One indication that there was a large increase in the numbers of African farmers marketing maize in sizable quantities may be gathered from the rise from 3,501 in 1965 to 7,392 in 1968 in the number of maize producers registered with the Grain Marketing Board.[8] A rough guess would be that the number of African registered maize producers increased from 2,500 in 1965 to 6,600 in 1968. Similar evidence exists for other crops.

Drawing together the data on the cash incomes and numbers of peasant semi-commercial farmers, one is led to the conclusion that, while many gained substantially from their first sorties into cash agriculture, those who were already established as semi-commercial farmers in 1964 can have gained very little, if anything, since then.[9]

Urban Informal Sector Incomes

Information on incomes in the urban informal sector is even more scarce than information on urban informal employment. From a variety of studies of self-employed workers and employers, one can derive an acceptable estimate of incomes at the higher end of the scale, but there are, as yet, no studies whose results are presented in a form which allow one to deduce the pattern of income distribution among informal sector employees.

In the section of Chapter 3 on urban informal employment, we estimated that as much as two-thirds of all employment in the urban informal sector, excluding domestic servants, consisted of work in which an individual was an employee of another, with a ratio of self-employment/wage employment/unpaid family workers of 1 : 1 : 1. From this it can be seen to be extremely important to have estimates of incomes among informal sector employees. Unfortunately, the only evidence that the author has is very impressionistic. I am reasonably sure, from discussions with agricultural officers in areas near the line of rail that the average monthly earnings of full-time employees of peasant farmers were in the region of K15 per month in 1974/5. With an allowance for the extra costs of living in urban areas rather than rural areas, this K15 in rural areas might have corresponded to an urban wage of K25. Where employees have some skills, as in building, this skill will be at a premium, so that among informal sector building employees, one might have expected to have observed average monthly wages of K30 or more in 1974/5—figures in line with Nat Tembo's studies of informal sector builders for the 1974 University College, London survey.

A final point to note is that an informal sector wage averaging K25-K30 per month in 1974/5 is, at present prices, no higher, and is probably slightly lower than average rural incomes valued at urban retail prices. Thus I will assume that average informal sector wages in 1974 were near K30 per month. The monthly earnings of unpaid family workers/'apprentices' are usually little more than board and lodging plus some pocket money, the total value of all of which I shall suppose to have been K15-K20 monthly.

For the informal construction sector, I have compared these estimated monthly incomes with estimates of the total annual value added within the sector, derived from detailed studies of informal housing areas in the 1973 Mwaziona and 1974 Chawama surveys. It is encouraging to find that, even where value added is estimated on a deliberately conservative basis, it is consistent with a labour force in informal construction activities divided one-third into unpaid family workers earning K15-K20 per month, one-third into wage employees, receiving K30 per month, and one-third into self-employed workers or employers earning an average of K60 per month.

Details of the average monthly incomes of informal sector employers are more readily available. Oberschall's various studies are the most useful in this respect. In a survey of small-scale trading enterprises in a Lusaka informal housing area in 1970, he found a median gross monthly income for the proprietors of K160.[10] Deducting an imputed interest and depreciation charge on the average capital of near K500 tied up in each business, the monthly income of the proprietors cannot have been much below K150. Oberschall's and Nat Tembo's estimates of marketeers' monthly incomes were somewhat lower than this, but were still near K100.

Callum Christie, in a paper to the Lusaka Economics Club, has suggested that the local organisation of the United National Independence Party (UNIP) operating within the main markets has prevented price competition from emerging to reduce trading incomes. Officials of UNIP enforce uniform prices, and typically raise the 'minimum' level of prices when competition reduces the market shares of the older, more established businesses. The UNIP local organisation, however, is only one barrier to competition in small trading; the amount of capital required to start up in business as a marketer or trader is another. Lower barriers to entry are involved in setting up as a 'tea-cart' pedlar. Mihalyi, in a 1972 study of two groups of pedlars in Lusaka, found that the initial capital required was of the order of K130, and that the typical range of monthly incomes was between K35 and K100.

The National Housing Authority's 1973 surveys of four site and service schemes produced average incomes among the self-employed which are in line with the figures given above. Their results are summarised in Table 4.3, below.

Table 4.3: Monthly Earnings of Site and Service Scheme Residents, 1973

Site and service scheme	Average earnings of self-employed (K)	Average earnings of wage employed (K)
Kaunda Square, Lusaka	106	81
Mtendere, Lusaka	71	67
(c.f. Doxiadis's 1968 survey of Lusaka)*	92	78)
Lubuto, Ndola	63	95
Chawama, Kafue	49	58

*NHA Report, Doxiadis Associates' study for the Lusaka Development Plan.

Drawing together this combination of inspired guesswork and patchy evidence about the urban informal sector, one can consider the form of income distribution that it implies for the sector as a whole. Figure 4.2, page 78, represents the results of the exercise, where we suppose that the median income of the self-employed was K60 per month in 1974.

Urban Formal Sector Incomes

As one would expect, the trend in formal sector incomes is well documented by the Central Statistical Office. The CSO statistics, summarised in Tables 4.4 and 4.5, pages 79 and 80, reveal that earnings rose

Figure 4.2: Income Distribution of Workers in the Urban Informal Sector (excluding Domestic Servants)

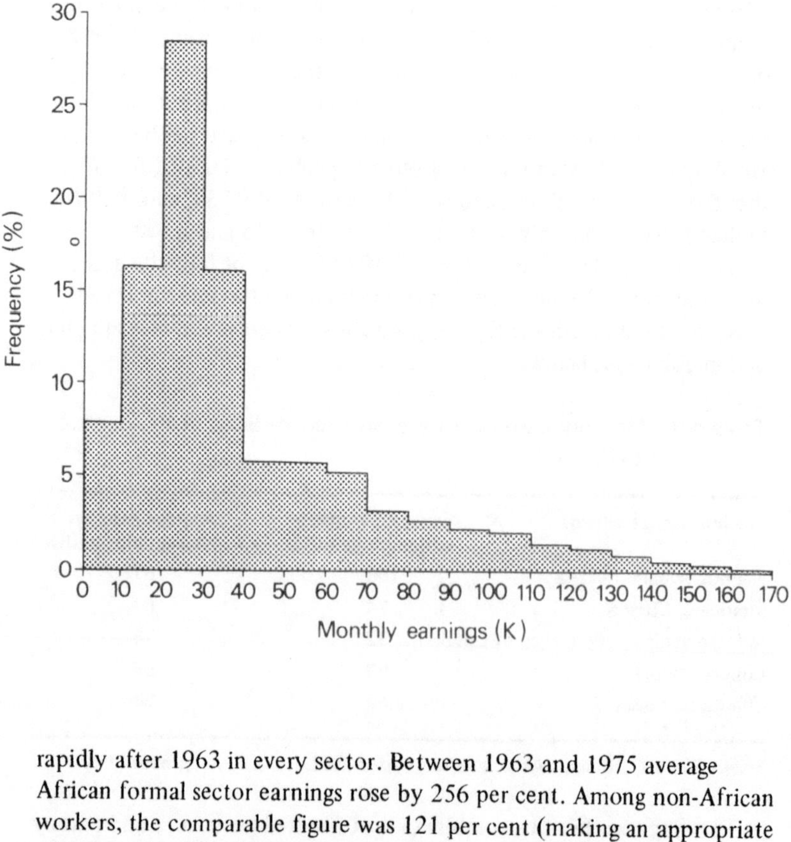

rapidly after 1963 in every sector. Between 1963 and 1975 average African formal sector earnings rose by 256 per cent. Among non-African workers, the comparable figure was 121 per cent (making an appropriate adjustment for the change that occurred in statistical definitions of employment categories in 1972).

In all sectors average earnings grew rapidly, although mining and construction were relative laggards. The disparity between mining wages and other wages narrowed only slowly (if one assumes that the 1975 figure for mining wages is something of an aberration), but, as we shall see in Chapter 6, there is little evidence that the differentials between the sectors in the wages paid for particular skills have narrowed. One must conclude therefore, that the changes on sectoral average wage differentials described in Table 4.4 reflect mainly changes in the structure of

Table 4.4: Average Earnings of African Workers, by Sector (K per annum), 1960-75

Year	Agriculture	Mining	Manufacturing	Construction	Electricity	Commerce	Transport	Services[a]	Services of which: Financial services	Services of which: Community services	Total	Low income[c] cost of living index (Jan. 1962=100.0)	Average earnings in Jan. 1962 (constant prices)	Public sector	Parastatal sector	Private sector
1960	120	570	236	236	210	232	292	256			272	100.3	271	—		—
1963	132	596	346	276	254	314	426	328			320	101.3	316	—		—
1964	176	732	406	286	320	388	482	392			382	104.5	366	—		—
1965	172	826	486	322	388	464	486	458			428	113.0	379	—		—
1966	190	934	478	332	456	488	688	526			480	124.5	386	476		482
1967	248	1,322	676	500	795	679	934	690			666	130.7	510	646		676
1968	352	1,248	635	649	689	744	946	720			713	144.9	492	689		727
1969	360	1,412	744	560	721	801	1,034	793			754	148.4	508	690		788
1970	348	1,543	802	609	816	795	1,211	789			928	152.3	609	724		1,048
									1,121	756						
1971[b]	383	1,636	1,005	707	829	836	1,424		1,217	844	1,033	161.5	640	899		1,108
1972[b]	407	1,554	910	718	822	883	1,348		1,100	871	1,017	170.2	597	914		1,056
Zambian workers																
1972	434	1,601	1,025	703	825	1,081	1,204		1,298	1,129	1,014	170.2	595	990		1,079
1973	419	1,685	1,064	724	922	1,147	1,292		1,328	1,318	1,135	181.0	627	1,144		1,129
1974	445	1,701	1,071	716	803	1,019	1,397		1,356	1,299	1,122	196.2	572	1,096		1,141
1975	453	1,478	1,179	764	1,042	1,018	1,834		1,641	1,259	1,140	215.9	528	1,147	1,381	899

[a]Excluding domestic service.
[b]These figures have been derived from the 1971 and 1972 statistics in such a way as to make the new bases of estimation employed in those years comparable with the figures for earlier years.
[c]Up to 1969 the indices were calculated from a 1962 base. After 1969 the published indices use a 1969 base year.
Source: *Monthly Digest of Statistics* (CSO, Lusaka).

Table 4.5: Average Earnings of Non-African Workers, by Sector (K per annum), 1960-75

Year	Sector: Agriculture	Mining	Manufacturing	Construction	Electricity	Commerce	Transport	Services[a]		Total	High income[c] cost of living index (Jan. 1962=100.0)	Average earnings in Jan. 1962 (constant prices)	Public sector	Private sector
1960	2,406	5,188	2,660	3,876	3,480	1,924	2,658	2,292		3,046	97.1	3,137	–	–
1963	2,650	5,128	2,704	2,940	3,684	2,092	2,892	2,456		3,170	102.1	3,105	–	–
1964	2,800	5,150	2,960	2,100	4,240	2,220	3,000	2,500		3,294	106.2	3,102	–	–
1965	2,364	5,378	3,128	3,510	4,274	2,478	3,078	2,900		3,498	110.7	3,160	–	–
1966	3,040	6,598	3,556	3,908	4,928	2,898	4,462	2,736		4,090	116.3	3,517	3,602	4,266
1967	3,142	7,608	4,581	4,650	5,736	3,986	3,766	2,704		4,458	122.2	3,648	3,370	4,858
1968	3,873	7,604	4,991	5,729	6,156	4,358	3,870	2,888		4,720	132.7	3,557	3,311	5,300
1969	4,144	8,174	5,154	5,693	6,750	4,591	4,018	3,826		4,369	138.5	3,516	3,374	5,487
1970	4,477	7,229	5,351	6,834	6,325	4,612	4,689	3,389		5,156	145.4	3,546	3,285	5,752
								of which						
								Financial services	Community services					
								5,296	2,704					
1971[b]	4,397	7,596	7,095	6,609	6,544	4,850	6,069	6,239	3,019	5,855	153.5	3,814	3,827	6,409
1972[b]	4,672	7,218	6,399	6,719	6,491	5,502	5,710	5,634	3,016	5,715	164.3	3,478	3,819	6,112
						Non-Zambian workers								
1972	3,148	5,014	5,248	4,377	5,483	4,680	4,143	6,339	3,303	4,548	164.3	2,768	3,598	4,826
1973	2,596	5,406	6,119	4,324	6,194	4,866	4,377	6,623	3,956	4,949	175.0	2,828	4,155	5,184
1974	2,602	6,629	5,866	4,371	6,062	5,066	4,653	6,947	4,168	5,389	191.2	2,819	4,391	5,681
												Public sector	Parastatal sector	Private sector
1975	2,524	6,784	5,657	6,868	7,835	5,316	7,377	7,528	3,859	5,572	207.5	3,768	6,799	5,272

[a]Excluding domestic service.
[b]These figures have been derived from the 1971 and 1972 statistics in such a way as to make the new bases of estimation employed in those years comparable with the figures for earlier years.
[c]Up to 1969 the indices were calculated from a 1962 base. After 1969 the published indices use a 1969 base year.
Source: *Monthly Digest of Statistics* (CSO, Lusaka).

the skills of African workers in different sectors. In real terms, the growing money incomes translate (using the Low Incomes Consumers' Price Index as a deflator for African earnings, and the High Incomes Index for non-African earnings) into a 67 per cent rise between 1963 and 1975 for African (Zambian) workers in general, and a 9 per cent rise for the average expatriate (non-Zambian).

Since independence, the real wages of African and non-African workers have followed a well defined step-like behaviour. African real wages have risen at the times of all major wage rounds in 1964, 1966-7 and 1970, discussed in more detail in Chapter 5. Non-African real earnings, however, appear to have risen only during the realignment of local and expatriate pay scales at the time of the Brown Commission in 1966, after which their recorded real earnings have remained virtually unaltered.[11] But the figures for expatriates fail to reflect their true financial position in as much as they make no systematic allowance for their various benefits in the form of inducement allowances, gratuities, etc. Taking these into consideration would probably add 15 per cent or more to the growth of expatriate real incomes between 1963 and 1972, making the true increase in this period 25-30 per cent for expatriates as a group.

From these figures one can observe that Zambian workers have gone far in closing the relative earnings gap between themselves and expatriates. If the expatriate/Zambian ratio in formal sector employment had remained at the 1963 level, then expatriate employment in 1976 would have been some 20,000 larger than it actually was. Thus it seems reasonable to suppose that 20,000 jobs, which in 1963 would have been done by expatriates, were being performed by Zambians in 1976. If one assumed further that these jobs were Zambianised at the full expatriate salary,[12] this would account for only one-third of the overall increase in African formal sector incomes in this period. In other words, at least 45 per cent out of the 67 per cent rise in African real earnings was not attributable to Zambianisation, implying that the underlying rate of increase in African real wages was twice that for expatriates.

In fact, the changing structure of expatriate employment since 1963 was such that, even without any increase in the expatriates' real wage scale, the average real expatriate wage would have been expected to have risen. Zambianisation has tended to displace relatively more of the lower-paid supervisory and technical expatriate staff than of those in posts requiring more skills. It seems possible that the changing composition of the expatriate work force has, by itself, accounted for over one-half of the growth in expatriates' average real wages between 1963 and 1976, with the result that, in jobs occupied by expatriates in 1976, the real wage may have grown at an annual rate of 1 per cent or less since 1963. An indication of the marked shift that was occurring between 1960 and 1976 in the formal sector earning power of the races can be found in the figures reproduced in Table 4.6, below.

Table 4.6: Total Formal Sector Earnings by Race*

Year	Africans	Non-Africans+ (K million)	Ratio non-African/ African total earnings
1960	66.4	100.5	1.51
1961	68.5	99.3	1.45
1962	69.8	103.1	1.48
1963	72.0	103.0	1.43
1964	90.5	104.4	1.16
1965	114.6	118.4	1.03
1966	136.6	118.1	0.87
1967	206.2	129.6	0.63
1968	232.3	136.5	0.59
1969	246.3	145.2	0.59
1970	320.5	141.4	0.44
1971	342.6	158.6	0.46
1972	344.5	148.5	0.43
	Zambians	non-Zambians	Ratio non-Zambian/ Zambian total earnings
1973	385.9	165.0	0.43
1974	394.9	179.6	0.45
1975	416.1	186.6	0.45

* In K million at current prices.
\+ Since these figures are derived from earlier tables, we do not include gratuities and other similar payments in the expatriates' total.

Regional Formal Sector Earnings

Just as striking as the racial and sectoral variations in wage levels are the variations between regions. Already, in Table 3.13, page 65, we have observed the extent of the regional biases in the location of wage employment, with the bulk of such employment located in the main administrative and industrial centres in Central and Copperbelt Provinces. The variation in regional formal sector earnings, shown in Table 4.7, page 83, only aggravates the already serious employment imbalance. In both the public and private sectors, the two provinces already the most favoured share the highest average wages per worker. Taking these figures together with the regional employment statistics given above, the full extent of the regional disparities in purchasing power can be estimated.

Table 4.7: Regional Distribution of Formal Sector Average Earnings in 1968 (K per annum)

Province	Sector: Public	Sector: Private	Sector: Overall	Share of Zambia's African formal sector employment (%)	Share of national African wage bill (%)
Central	752	754	753	28.4	28.0
Copperbelt	757	954	935	43.3	53.0
Eastern	717	262	591	4.6	3.6
Luapula	642	641	642	2.4	2.0
Northern	422	485	430	4.5	2.5
North Western	444	291	404	2.1	1.1
Southern	482	535	516	11.4	7.7
Western	522	392	483	3.3	2.1
Whole country	689	788	754		

Table 4.7 provides proof of the inability of the government to stimulate the formal sector away from the line of rail. Furthermore the table indicates why, in the absence of large structural changes, such as the opening up of the area alongside the new Tan Zam railway line, Zambia's outlying provinces stand little chance of achieving rapid and sustained economic development; for their local markets are too small for all but the smallest manufacturing industries. If we compare the neighbouring Copperbelt and North Western Provinces, for example, the latter had in 1968 28 per cent of the population of the former, but only 4.5 per cent of its formal sector employment, and a mere 2.1 per cent of its African wage bill. It can be small wonder that the North Western Province finds itself highly dependent on goods brought in from the main Copperbelt towns.

Wages and Inflation

In view of the remarkable increase in money wages that we have observed to have taken place over the past few years, it is interesting to ask exactly how this has affected the cost of living and how it might have contributed to the erosion of real wage levels through an interaction of wage and price inflation. *A priori*, one would expect the effect of higher wages on the cost of living to have been rather muted, both as a cost-push and a demand-pull factor behind domestic inflation. On the cost-push side, a majority of Zambia's formal sector employment is to be found in industries whose selling price bears only a weak relation to local production costs – the mining and agricultural sectors are the most obvious examples – or in sectors, like government administration or social services, whose products are made available without charge. On the demand-pull side, a large proportion of Zambia's consumer goods are supplied from abroad (from Table 3.14, pages 67-8, it would appear that, directly and indirectly, imports account for nearly 60 per cent of the value of total consumption expenditure). Since, in addition, the Zambian market had until 1975 remained very open to imports, changes in domestic demand conditions were reflected more in the volume of consumer goods imports than in the local price level.

Table 4.8: Sources of Inflation in Zambia, 1964-8 (values given are percentage increases over the two-year periods shown)

	1964-6	1966-8
Increases in consumer prices owing to cost-push factors of which	9.9	13.2
increases in wages	5.0	7.8
increases in import prices	3.2	3.6
increases in import freight costs	1.7	1.8
Increases in combined high- and low-income cost of living indices	14.2	15.6
Percentage of rise in cost of living attributable to cost-push factors	70	85
Direct increase in consumer prices as a result of rerouting following Rhodesia's UDI	3.6	3.6

Sources: R. Jolly and M. Williams, *Fiscal, Monetary and Cost-Push Factors*, Table 7; and, for the estimate of the impact of the rerouting of imports following Rhodesia's UDI, J. Fry, University of Zambia, Economics Discussion Paper, 'The Cost of Living in Zambia'.

The only detailed analysis of the causes of Zambian inflation tends to confirm the *a priori* expectations just described.[13] Rising wages, as a cost-push and demand-pull cause of inflation, are identified as the most important single contributory factor behind Zambia's recent inflation, but on average, a 10 per cent increase in wage rates gave rise to only a 2.5 per cent increase in the cost of living. Jolly and Williams chose to consider wage increases as reflecting cost-push pressures, rather than any demand-pull influences from employers having to bid up wage rates to attract more labour. Table 4.8, page 84, summarises their main conclusions regarding the sources of domestic inflation between 1964 and 1968. When one remembers that, between 1964 and 1968, African wages grew at an average annual rate of 17 per cent (or 37 per cent over each two-year period), and non-African wages grew at 9.6 per cent per annum (20 per cent over each two-year period), one has to conclude that an annual rise in the cost of living of a mere 3.2 per cent, on account of wages alone, was a very creditable performance.

Income Distribution

In Figures 4.1 and 4.2, pages 73 and 78, we have presented estimates of the distribution of incomes in traditional agriculture and the urban informal sector. Unfortunately, the nature of the data means that, whereas the distribution of incomes within traditional agriculture is described in terms of household incomes, the distribution in the informal sector is based upon individual members of the employed labour force. The lack of uniformity in measurement units is a problem which is going to plague any attempt to derive a comprehensive indication of national income distribution. Household budget surveys take households as their units of measurement; income tax data take the individual tax payers as their units of measurement, but since very few, if any, tax payers opt for separate assessments of husbands' and wives' incomes, the income tax data may be assumed to be similar to data collected on the basis of households. Township surveys differ with regard to their basis of measurement. Some collect information only for heads of household, others collect it for the entire adult population. Finally one has social security statistics, such as those derived from Zambia National Provident Fund (ZNPF) returns, which are collected strictly on the basis of wage earners.

In Tables 4.9 and 4.10, pages 86 and 87, the author has brought together the results of all the main published and unpublished studies of the distribution of income among low-income and high-income individuals and households in Zambia. The statistics in Tables 4.9 and 4.10 must be interpreted carefully, for, while urban areas are well covered in the results that are presented, rural areas are included only in the coverage of income tax and Provident Fund statistics, and even then, it is only the large-scale commercial farming sector that is represented. In addition, one must note that, whereas informal sector workers are well represented in the various township and household budget surveys, they

Table 4.9: Income Distribution Among Low-Income Earners (in % frequency)

	Surveys						
Monthly incomes in range (K)	1966-7* of Lusaka low-cost informal townships	1966-8 of low-income urban budget survey (incomes)	1966-8 of low-income urban budget survey (expenditures)	1968* ZNPF returns	1973-4* of Lusaka low-cost informal townships	1973 of urban site and service schemes	1974* ZNPF returns
0-10	1%	10%	2%	—	2%	1%	—
10-20	10%	3%	7%	10%	2%	3%	7%
20-30	37%	8%	11%	25%	5%	12%	16%
30-40	26%	13%	17%	12%	19%	16%	11%
40-50	15%	11%	16%	8%	24%	10%	11%
50-60	4%	10%	12%	19%	13%	10%	9%
60-70	3%	10%	9%	8%	13%	4%	8%
70-80	1%	7%	7%	4%	6%	10%	7%
80-90	1%	6%	4%	15%	5%	9%	5%
90-100	1%	4%	3%	15%	3%	5%	4%
100-110	1%	4%	3%	15%	2%	4%	3%
110-120	1%	2%	2%	15%	1%	5%	2%
120-130	1%	2%	1%	15%	2%	3%	16%
130-140	1%	2%	1%	15%	1%	2%	16%
140-150	1%	1%	1%	15%	—	4%	16%
150-160	1%	1%	1%	15%	—	—	16%
160+	1%	5%	3%	15%	2%	13%	16%
Coverage of survey	Average of Kalingalinga, Nguluwe and New Kanyama surveys. The first two covered only heads of household; the last covered only lodgers. However, all three gave very similar results.	Households in lost-cost housing areas, chosen from all major urban centres in Zambia as well as from some minor urban centres.	See previous column	Majority of lower paid wage employees.	Average of 1973 Mwaziona survey, covering heads of household, and 1974 Chawama survey, covering labour force. Both gave similar results.	National Housing Authority survey in three towns.	Vast majority of lower paid wage employees.
Sample size	400	2,500	2,500	150,000	1,200	200	250,000

*These results exclude the unemployed.

Sources: As for Tables 3.6 and 4.3. Also CSO, 1966-8 *Urban Budget Survey*; and, for ZNPF returns, author's own analysis of ZNPF monthly contributions.

Table 4.10: Income Distribution Among High-Income Earners

1962-4 income tax returns		1970-1 income tax returns	
Income in range (K)	Number of potential tax payers	Income in range* (K)	Number of potential tax payers*
1,600-2,000+	10,000	1,500-2,000	43,000
2,000-2,400+	8,000	2,000-2,500	21,000
2,400-3,000+	9,000	2,500-3,000	8,500
3,000-4,000+	8,000	3,000-3,500	5,300
4,000-5,000	5,365	3,500-4,000	3,700
5,000-6,000	2,497	4,000-5,500	6,500
6,000-8,000	1,576	5,500-7,500	5,000
8,000-10,000	318	7,500-10,000	2,800
10,000-12,000	131	10,000-11,500	700
12,000-14,000	60	11,500-16,500	600
14,000-16,000	44	16,500-21,500	200
16,000-18,000	26	21,500+	160
18,000-20,000	5		
20,000-30,000	24		
30,000-40,000	4		
40,000-50,000	—		
50,000-60,000	1		
Total: approx.	45,000	Total: approx.	97,500

* The pre-tax incomes have been estimated from statistics of tax payers; therefore, the income ranges and numbers in each range are only approximate.

\+ Up to K4,000, not all married people pay income tax; therefore a multiplying factor has been used to estimate the number of married potential tax payers from the number of single taxpayers.

Source: Commissioner of Taxes *Reports* for 1963, 1964 and 1971.

will be considerably under-represented in the Provident Fund and income tax statistics.

One major problem which one has to face when interpreting Table 4.9 concerns the definition of low income. The Provident Fund statistics, for example, are derived from details of the contributions paid by, or on behalf of, individual members of the ZNPF. All wage earners are required by law to belong to the ZNPF, unless they belong to accredited superannuation schemes. This, in effect, means that the coverage of the ZNPF statistics is somewhat patchy, even as regards formal sector workers. In 1968, there appears to have been the additional complication that some employers were late in submitting returns, so that the distribution for that year overstates the importance of copper miners, which explains the large number of ZNPF members recorded as earning K50-K60 per month.

In 1974, the ZNPF's major omissions were those employees who were covered by pension schemes. Since pension schemes cover only more highly paid workers, we may conclude that the ZNPF returns correspond to a somewhat downward biased reflection of formal sector income distribution for employees receiving less than K200 per month (at which income level, most workers belong to pension schemes). The downward bias is caused partly by the higher proportion of more highly paid employees who belong to pension schemes, but it is also a result of the fact that ZNPF contributions are paid on the basis of basic wages, rather than total earnings, though this may be offset slightly by the small numbers of workers who choose voluntarily to pay larger ZNPF contributions than they are obliged to.

The surveys of incomes in low-cost informal housing areas will also be biased downwards, since more prosperous, or longer established, low-income workers tend to move out of high density informal housing to high or medium density formal housing. To a much lesser extent, the same downward bias will apply to the urban budget surveys, which were carried out only in low-cost, high density housing areas, and thus excluded those low-income households living in medium density housing. However, below K100, one might fairly take the urban budget surveys to give a good representation of the true urban household income distribution.

If one takes the urban budget surveys to be the basis of income distribution at low income levels, one still has the problem of deciding whether one should rely upon income or expenditure data. This problem is particularly important where incomes are very low, since at these levels, the divergence between income and expenditure distributions becomes very large indeed. Furthermore, close study of the Urban Budget Survey report throws up some remarkable results, such as that the average monthly consumption expenditure of households earning less than K10 per month was K48.76, on top of which another K5.30 of gifts and loans were given! Since income data allegedly included as part of income all borrowings and loans, the only possible explanation for expenditures being at least five times as large as incomes must be that the workers in question were dissaving, and that for the month that they were being surveyed, they were temporarily unemployed, or earning very low incomes. Over a longer period of time, it would seem reasonable to suppose that their average household monthly income was similar to their average monthly expenditure. Accordingly, for incomes below K50 per month, I shall suppose that the expenditure pattern, rather than the incomes pattern, represents the true 'long-period-income distribution'. For incomes between K50 and K100 per month, I shall suppose that the incomes pattern represents the true 'long-period-income distribution'. For incomes over K100 per month, I shall assume a steadily growing downward bias in the Budget Survey figures, up to the point where income tax statistics can be used as a cross check. Unfortunately, the income tax statistics in Table 4.10 cover different periods from the low-income studies summarised in Table 4.9, and thus one has to adjust for the growth in incomes and numbers of the better paid to derive estimates for 1967 and 1974.

Assuming that the income tax statistics can be taken to correspond closely to household income statistics for high-income householders,[14] the procedure described above should yield the distribution of income among urban households in 1967. For 1974, however, we do not have any budget surveys to help us. The most useful guide we have is that, in 1966-8, when one compares cumulative frequencies of the ZNPF returns with our revised Budget Survey results one finds that at almost every percentile, the Budget Survey income is approximately 1.40 times the ZNPF income. Allowing for income growth during the period between the field work for the Urban Budget Surveys and the ZNPF tabulation, it would appear to be true to say that if one multiplies all income ranges for the ZNPF returns by a factor of 1.35, one will derive the corrected Budget Survey pattern of income distribution. This is what we do to estimate the 1974 urban income distribution in Table 4.11, page 90. In Table 4.12, page 91, Table 39 is converted into frequency distributions, and from this one can derive Figure 4.3, page 92, expressing 1968 and 1974 urban household income distribution in terms of Lorenz curves.

Unfortunately the margin of error in our statistics on income distribution is necessarily fairly large, so that it would be unwise to place much weight on the conclusion that can be drawn from Figure 4.3, page 92, that the inequality in urban incomes has decreased slightly between 1968 and 1974. However, it is significant that both the 1968 and 1974 statistics are in rough agreement that the top 1 per cent of urban households receive 8 per cent of urban incomes; the top 2 per cent receive 13 per cent of total urban incomes; the top 5 per cent receive 24 per cent; the top 10 per cent receive 36 per cent; the top 20 per cent receive 51 per cent; and the top 50 per cent receive 80 per cent of all urban household incomes. The poorest 50 per cent therefore receive only 20 per

Table 4.11: Urban Income Distribution, 1968 and 1974

Monthly income (K)	Number of households 1968	1974
0-10	4,000	2,000
10-20	12,000	8,000
20-30	16,000	23,000
30-40	27,000	35,000
40-50	25,000	23,000
50-60	20,000	22,000
60-70	18,000	21,000
70-80	13,000	18,000
80-90	12,000	18,000
90-100	11,000	17,500
100-110	10,000	16,500
110-120	9,000	15,500
120-130	8,000	14,000
130-140	7,500	14,000
140-150	6,500	13,500
150-160	5,500	12,000
160-170	5,000	10,500
170-180	4,000	9,000
180-190	3,000	7,000
190-200	2,500	5,500
200-250	8,000	13,000
250-300	6,500	8,000
300-400	6,500	9,000
400-500	4,000	5,250
500-600	2,000	3,000
600-700	1,500	2,000
700-800	1,000	1,500
800-900	600	900
900-1,000	400	750
Over 1,000	500	1,100
Total number of households	250,000	350,000

cent of total urban incomes.

Estimates of rural income distributional statistics along the lines of those described in Figure 4.1 are even less reliable than our estimates of urban income distribution. However, taking Figure 4.1 to represent the

Table 4.12: Urban Incomes Distribution, 1968 and 1974 (in percentages)

	1968				1974			
Monthly Income (K)	Proportion of total households (%)	Cumulative proportion of total households (%)	Proportion of total incomes (%)	Cumulative proportion of total incomes (%)	Proportion of total households (%)	Cumulative proportion of total households (%)	Proportion of total incomes (%)	Cumulative proportion of total incomes (%)
0-10	1.6	1.6	0.1	0.1	0.6	0.6	0.02	0.02
10-20	4.8	6.4	0.6	0.7	2.3	2.9	0.27	0.3
20-30	6.4	12.8	1.4	2.1	6.6	9.5	1.3	1.6
30-40	10.8	23.6	3.3	5.4	9.9	19.4	2.8	4.4
40-50	10.0	33.6	4.0	9.4	6.6	26.0	2.3	6.7
50-60	8.0	41.6	3.9	13.3	6.3	32.2	2.7	9.4
60-70	7.2	48.8	4.1	17.4	6.0	38.3	3.1	12.5
70-80	5.2	54.0	3.4	20.8	5.3	43.6	3.1	15.6
80-90	4.8	58.8	3.6	24.4	5.1	48.7	3.5	19.1
90-100	4.4	63.2	3.7	28.1	5.0	53.7	3.8	22.9
100-110	4.0	67.2	3.7	31.8	4.7	58.4	3.9	26.8
110-120	3.6	70.8	3.6	35.4	4.4	62.8	4.0	30.8
120-130	3.2	74.0	3.5	38.9	4.0	66.8	3.9	34.7
130-140	3.0	77.0	3.6	42.5	4.0	70.8	4.3	39.0
140-150	2.6	79.6	3.3	45.8	3.9	74.7	4.4	43.4
150-160	2.2	81.8	3.0	48.8	3.4	78.1	4.2	47.6
160-170	2.0	83.8	2.9	51.7	3.0	81.1	3.9	51.5
170-180	1.6	85.4	2.5	54.2	2.6	83.7	3.6	55.1
180-190	1.2	86.6	2.0	56.2	2.0	85.7	2.9	58.0
190-200	1.0	87.6	1.7	57.9	1.6	87.3	2.4	60.4
200-250	3.2	90.8	6.3	64.2	3.6	90.9	6.6	67.0
250-300	2.6	93.4	6.3	70.5	2.3	93.2	5.0	72.0
300-400	2.6	96.0	8.0	78.5	2.6	95.8	7.1	79.1
400-500	1.6	97.6	6.3	84.8	1.5	97.3	5.3	84.4
500-600	0.8	98.4	3.9	88.7	0.9	98.2	3.7	88.1
600-700	0.6	99.0	3.4	92.1	0.6	98.8	2.9	91.0
700-800	0.4	99.4	2.6	94.7	0.4	99.2	2.5	93.5
800-900	0.25	99.6	1.8	96.5	0.25	99.5	1.7	95.2
900-1,000	0.15	99.8	1.3	97.8	0.21	99.7	1.6	96.8
Over 1,000	0.20	100.0	2.2	100.0	0.31	100.0	3.2	100.0

Figure 4.3: Lorenz Curves of Urban Household Income Distribution

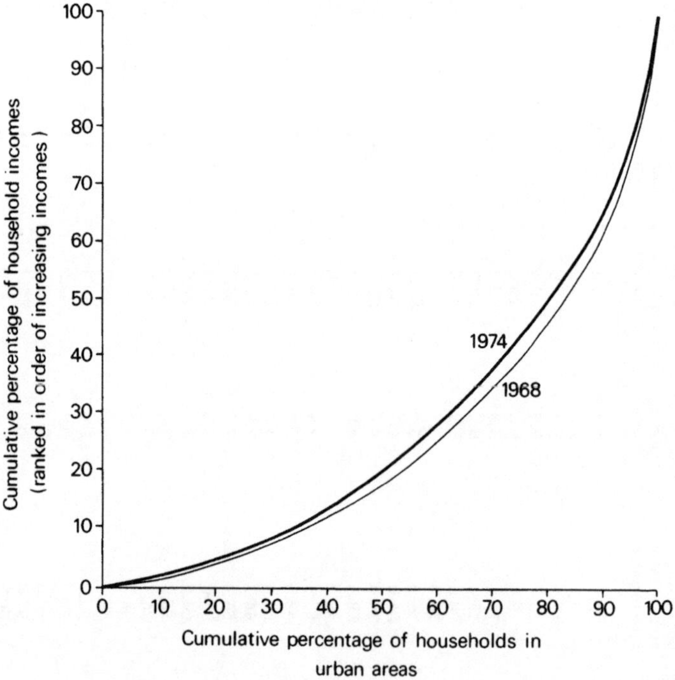

Table 4.13: Household Income Distribution, 1970

Share of total income received by the top	National income distribution (%)	Urban income distribution (%)
1% of all households	13	8
2% of all households	19	13
5% of all households	33	24
10% of all households	48	36
20% of all households	63	51
50% of all households	80	80

distribution of rural incomes in 1976, and adjusting for the change in prices since 1970, one can derive Table 4.13, above, contrasting the overall national pattern of distribution of household incomes in 1970 with the pattern of income distribution in urban areas alone.

This represents the limit beyond which it would be inappropriate, and probably misleading, to try to draw further conclusions from the restricted data available on incomes. Yet there remains one final question which ought to be considered in the present discussion; this is whether our belief that cash incomes and their distribution have changed for the better with growing urbanisation remains true when we examine non-monetary components of the standard of living. As regards social services, like education or health facilities, there can be little doubt that the overall position has improved substantially since the early 1960s; but it is less obvious that the changes that have occurred with respect to the security of land tenure, the provision of sanitation services and water supplies, or the quality and quantity of housing, have been for the better.

To answer this question satisfactorily on the national basis would require the sort of microdata which are virtually unobtainable, except in the 1969 Population Census; and in that particular source the data are often too aggregated for our purposes, and, even where they are not, there are no statistics for other dates to use as a basis for comparison. Therefore, one is drawn back to the excellent University College, London survey, for which John Collins prepared a set of indicators of tenure, water supply, sanitation, rooms, walling and roofing for Lusaka in 1957, 1963, 1969 and 1973. Collins estimated the numbers of households whose housing met certain lower or upper threshold standards concerning their living conditions. For example, households with their own private taps are considered to be above the upper threshold for water supplies, those sharing a tap are between the upper and lower thresholds, and those below the lower threshold get their water from other sources.

From Table 4.14 one can observe that for Lusaka as a whole the improvement in living conditions has been only gradual. But if, as seems likely, most of those with poorer living conditions are in the rural areas, then one is entitled to deduce that the increasing urbanisation of recent years has been accompanied by a gradual improvement in living conditions alongside a more dramatic increase in real cash incomes.

Conclusions

The most important conclusion to be derived from the discussion in this chapter is that there is much more to the growth of incomes and employment in Zambia than the well known and well documented expansion in formal sector wage employment and formal sector wage

Table 4.14: Lusaka Housing Indicators, 1957-73 (% of Lusaka households*)

Indicator		1957 (%)	1963 (%)	1969 (%)	1973 (%)
Tenure	Above UT+	12	14	23	24
	Between	50	62	40	34
	Below LT+	38	24	37	42
Water	Above UT	23	33	29	32
	Between	59	51	38	31
	Below LT	18	16	33	37
Sanitation	Above UT	23	33	31	34
	Between	35	38	39	33
	Below LT	42	29	30	33
Rooms (number per person)	Above UT	21	23	31	38
	Between	35	41	31	35
	Below LT	44	36	38	27
Walling	Above UT	59	62	57	53
	Between	27	24	35	43
	Below LT	13	13	8	4
Roofing	Above UT	65	79	80	97
	Between	16	8	13	1
	Below LT	19	13	7	2
Total°	Above UT	37	41	42	47
	Between	37	37	33	29
	Below LT	26	22	25	24

* All percentages refer to households, except for the number of rooms per person, which is in terms of the number of dwellings.

\+ Our three categories are 'Above Upper Threshold', 'Between Thresholds', and 'Below Lower Threshold'.

° This total represents merely the arithmetic mean of all six indicator percentages.

levels since 1963. The formal sector's development has certainly been dramatic, but not as dramatic as the structural change that the formal sector's transformation has wrought on the labour market as a whole.

With the ending of the colonial system of controls on labour mobility, workers from Zambia's rural areas were able to move to the attractive income opportunities available in the main towns. The inflow of workers exceeded by a large margin the capacity of the formal sector to provide employment, and a substantial proportion of the immigrants had to accept informal sector employment, if they were not to be unemployed. Thus, for a worker considering leaving the rural areas, where the deterioration in the barter terms of trade facing peasant farmers has eroded much of the benefit from higher agricultural output, income expectations in the urban areas have become increasingly influenced by the level of incomes in the informal urban sector.

For an unskilled rural worker without any capital, the structure of job opportunities in the towns has shifted so strongly towards the informal sector that it now seems fair to say that, at K40 per month, his expected earnings in town provide a standard of living no better than that obtainable from small-scale peasant agriculture. For an unskilled rural worker with capital, the situation varies from province to province, but where, as in the southern half of the country, cattle or agricultural implements can provide their owners with attractive financial returns, agriculture can yield at least as high incomes as small-scale urban enterprises. It is only for skilled or well-educated workers that the urban job market is almost invariably more remunerative than the rural alternative, though even in this case, workers are increasingly having to accept long periods of unemployment before they can find a job which they feel is appropriate to their educational qualifications.

The recent attainment of equilibrium in the market for unskilled labour has already been reflected in a diminution in the rate of growth of Zambia's urban population. In view of this chapter's demonstration that Zambia's present development strategy is likely to reduce the rate of formal sector employment growth, one must suppose that the flow of migrants from the rural to the urban areas is likely to continue to decrease over the next few years.

Notes

1. *The Universities of Nottingham and Zambia Agricultural Labour Productivity Investigation Reports*, 1-6, published between 1969 and 1973.
2. *UNZALPI Report No. 3*, pp. 7 and 8.
3. *Southern Province of Zambia: Prospects of Regional Development* (Gesellschaft für Regionale Strukturentwicklung eV, Bonn, 1971).
4. *The Importance of Traditional Agriculture in Zambia*, mimeo (Planning Office, Lusaka, 1970).
5. In Table 3.3, 9.5 acres corresponds to an income of K300 in Figure 4.1. Thus, in Southern Province we would expect to find annual cash incomes of over K300 in the case of 36.5% of all traditional farmers, equivalent to 46% of those traditional farmers marketing cash crops; 3% of all Southern Province

farmers, or 4.5% of all Southern Province cash farmers would be expected to earn over K1,200 per annum from cash sales.

6. See 'An Investigation into the change in the terms of trade between the rural and urban sectors of Zambia', *African Social Research*, 12, December (1971), pp. 95-110. Note that the use of the term 'rural-urban terms of trade' is slightly misleading in the context of the discussion that follows. The strictly correct terminology would be 'the terms of trade facing Zambian peasant farmers in their cash transactions with the rest of the world economy'. Since the majority of peasant farmers' cash purchases are of manufactured goods, such as clothes, which are produced in the urban areas of Zambia, 'rural-urban terms of trade' is a useful form of shorthand for our purposes.

7. See 'Rural-Urban Terms of Trade, 1960-73: A Note', *African Social Research*, 19 June (1975), pp. 730-8.

8. *Annual Report* (Grain Marketing Board, 1969). A registered producer of maize undertakes to sell a minimum of 16 200-lb bags of maize each year.

9. The author discusses this further in his note in *African Social Research*, 19, June (1975).

10. A. Oberschall, 'African Traders and Small Business in Lusaka', *African Social Research*, 16 December (1973), pp. 474-502.

11. One has, of course, to make an appropriate adjustment to Table 4.5 to allow for the change from 'Non-Africans' to 'Non-Zambians' in 1972.

12. This is surely a considerable overestimate. See, for example, the comparison of Zambian and expatriate salaries for similar jobs given in the 1966 *Manpower Report.* Remember also that Zambians do not receive gratuities and other such perks.

13. See R. Jolly and M. Williams, *Fiscal, Monetary and Cost-Push Factors in the Zambian Economy, 1964-1970*, mimeo (Planning Office, Lusaka, 1970).

14. In other words, we are making the (reasonable) assumption that, in the vast majority of cases, the unit upon which income tax is assessed is the household.

5 ISSUES IN WAGE DETERMINATION—THE HISTORICAL BACKGROUND

Although wage employment accounts for only 20 to 25 per cent of total employment in Zambia, it is easy to understand why a disproportionate amount of interest in income distribution is focused upon the manner of determination of wage levels. Data on wages in the modern sector are more accurate and more detailed than the data available for other sectors; and wage incomes account for as much as three-quarters of total labour incomes in Zambia. The disparity between wage and non-wage incomes therefore lies at the heart of the unequal distribution of personal incomes in Zambia.

The analysis of wage determination is also of particular interest to the social scientist, since the level of wages cannot adequately be explained in terms of orthodox classical or neoclassical theories. As our earlier chapters on the distribution of incomes indicate, wage levels in the modern sector of Zambia are well above both subsistence wages and the marginal product of labour in the non-wage sector, even where one allows for a reasonable margin to compensate for the necessary extra costs of urban as against rural life.

One recently developed theory which attempts to meet some of these objections to the orthodox view is the 'efficiency wage' approach. This argues that there is a range of wage levels over which higher wages are profitable to an employer in the sense that increased labour costs result in even greater increases (as a result of better nutrition) in labour efficiency. Hence, observed wages may be unrelated to alternative earnings in agriculture. In low-income, low-wage, land-scarce areas, such as parts of India, there is strong empirical evidence to support the efficiency wage hypothesis. But in Zambia, the steady rise in real wages over a long period of time, the existence of considerable sectoral wage differentials, and the contrast between wages in Zambia and in other neighbouring states, all militate against accepting this particular explanation of wage determination.

Another new theory, mentioned briefly in Chapter 1, is the 'labour turnover' model, which stresses the employer's incentive to pay a premium to workers to stabilise the labour force and reduce labour turnover. At the end of the present chapter I shall demonstrate that the labour turnover approach can be shown to go far in explaining the distribution of wages and skills in different sectors of the Zambian economy.

With the exception of the one theoretical section at the end of this chapter, the present chapter and Chapter 6 are concerned mainly with what might be called a micro-economic, institutional line of analysis. Wages and their manner of determination will be considered not only from the point of view of the economic factors at work, but also in terms of the 'institutional' social and political pressures that have impinged strongly upon wage awards over the past 15 years. As a framework for the discussion, it is convenient to study wage fixing in terms of four differentials which, between them, determine the distribution of wages in Zambia. The four are the differentials between the earnings of (i) expatriate and local workers, (ii) rural and urban workers, (iii) workers in different sectors, and (iv) skilled and unskilled workers.

The bulk of these two chapters will be concerned with arguing that only a part, often a small part, of these four differentials can be explained in purely economic terms. But, before presenting our detailed argument, it is useful first to run quickly over the main events affecting wage determination in Zambia in the recent past. Table 5.1, page 99, summarises the events that have occurred since 1961 (up to 1976). However, one can probably understand the changing emphases of industrial relations and wage determination better if one considers the labour history of Zambia as being divided into three eras. The first era, up to 1961, corresponded to the period in which African and non-African workers were employed on wage scales, and in employment categories, which bore few points of overlap between the races. The second era, from 1961 to 1967, covering the last three years of colonial rule and the first three years of political independence, saw wage determination dominated by a gradual movement towards a unified non-racial pay scale in all sectors. The third era, from 1967 to the present day, covers the only period during which wage fixing took place in an atmosphere virtually free of any racially based inequalities in the pay scale.

The Struggle for African Advancement: Period Before 1961

Before the development of the mining industry in the late 1920s, formal sector wages remained at levels close to subsistence agricultural incomes. Poll taxation and recruitment agencies ensured that the required supply of labour would be forthcoming at low wages, without employers having to resort to offering financial inducements.

The first stage of the development of the copper mines coincided with the Depression, so that the mines, relying upon the stock of migrant

Table 5.1: Man-Days Lost through Strikes, Growth of Earnings and Diary of Events

Year	% growth in average African earnings over previous year	Man-days of work lost through strikes	Main events of significance in sphere of industrial relations
(1960)	(5.6)	(7,507)	
1961	5.9	19,640	General statutory minimum wages became effective for the first time in January 1961. A non-racial Civil Service was created in November 1961. Rhodesia Railways also adopted a non-racial pay scale.
1962	4.9	541,894	Considerable unrest on mines over African advancement and pay. *Morison Commission* set up in May 1962 to recommend new mining pay scales.
1963	6.0	409,559	Major stoppage at Mufulira Mine over incentive bonuses. Large rise in General Minimum Wage. *Hadow Commission* on Civil Service salaries appointed September 1963.
1964	19.4	125,738	*Hadow Commission* reported, and produced a unified Civil Service pay structure. On the mines, African workers secured a pay rise as the price for accepting a dual mining wage structure. Considerable unrest by European miners, who finally changed to monthly terms and secured higher pay. For the first time, minimum wages were fixed in agriculture.
1965	12.0	22,493	A major strike on the copper mines was averted by a constitutional wrangle in the (African) Zambia Mineworkers' Union (ZMU).
1966	12.1	579,406	In January, the ZMU signed a pay agreement which proved unacceptable to its members. The *Brown Commission* was established in April to investigate miners' grievances and reported in August. The *Whelan Commission* on Civil Service salaries was also appointed in April.
1967	38.7	46,088	Peace on the mines. Many rises in statutory minimum wages. Some strikes by local authority workers occurred when the government reduced their pay award. Three African mine unions merged to form the Mineworkers' Union of Zambia (MUZ).

Year	% growth in average African earnings over previous year	Man-days of work lost through strikes	Main events of significance in sphere of industrial relations
1968	7.1	65,898	Marked by some further industrial action by local authority workers and unofficial strikes on Zambia Railways in support of a pay claim.
1969	5.8	21,069	The mines and MUZ agreed to co-operate on a new job evaluation exercise to arrive at a new job grading structure. In March a *Salaries Commission* for the Civil Service was announced. In August a pay freeze was ordered, and in December a limit of 5% on annual wage increases was approved at the Second National Convention.
1970	23.1	122,951	A serious strike affected the railways. There was also a large-scale unofficial strike by teachers over the delay in implementing new conditions. Local authority workers' unrest continued over their 1967 award. In September, the MUZ and the mines reached an agreement on job grading which led to dissatisfaction from the workers who were downgraded.
1971	11.3	18,894	Threats of unofficial strikes on the mines by workers dissatisfied with the 1970 agreement averted only by the detention of the dissidents' leaders. There were increases in many statutory minimum wages. The *O'Riordan Salaries Commission* reported in May, awarding sizable wage increases to public servants.
1972	- 1.7	20,874	The tail-end of the 1970-2 wage round, with increases in many statutory minimum wages.
1973	11.9	5,663	Copper miners won a 20% wage increase, to be spread over three years. Government attempts to centralise the trade union movement aroused strong opposition.
1974	- 1.1	38,650	The Industrial Relations Act was brought into force in April. The *Mwanakatwe Salaries Commission* was appointed.
1975	1.6	51,007	The *Mwanakatwe Commission* granted a substantial pay increase to civil servants, and was followed immediately by a wage award for miners.
1976	Not available	6,527	The Mwanakatwe award was taken as a basis for wage rises in other sectors. Both local and expatriate miners were awarded wage increases after the devaluation of the Kwacha.

workers who had come to depend upon wage employment to provide most of their needs, were able to dispense with formal recruitment, and reduce real money wages, without inducing a labour shortage. The miners' attempt in 1935 to strike in protest against higher taxation was met by force, and failed completely to prevent the real disposable money income of mineworkers from falling further below the pre-Depression level. Yet, even during the Depression there were indications that the mining companies, attempting to emulate the Union Minière in Katanga by reducing labour turnover and increasing labour efficiency, were prepared to raise the real cost of labour to themselves in order to 'stabilise' their work force. Although real money wages fell during the 1930s, the value of housing, rations and other fringe benefits provided for African mineworkers rose appreciably.

The turning point as regards African wages came in 1940. The Second World War increased the demands being made upon the mining industry, while the absence of many white miners in the armed forces compelled the mining companies to rely heavily upon African workers to perform some of the semi-skilled jobs customarily reserved for Europeans. Furthermore, the British Colonial Office had come, by the late 1930s, to favour a policy of greater political and economic rights for African workers. In the face of strong opposition from local white settlers, the Colonial Office in 1932 issued the famous Passfield Memorandum, asserting the paramountcy of African over settler interests. During the late 1930s Labour Departments were established in most British African colonies to deal with labour matters affecting both African and European workers, and thus to attempt to ensure a greater balance between the interests of the two groups of workers.

The Colonial Office, in these matters, remained true to its general policy of seeking to channel the economic and political grievances of the African labour force in different directions, so that, as in Britain, workers' industrial and labour grievances could be prevented from leading to serious political conflict. In furtherance of this policy, the Colonial Office favoured the liberalisation of employment opportunities for Africans and supported the principle of African advancement. This also helps to explain why it was that in 1946 the colonial government took the lead in encouraging the formation of African trade unions, since it wanted to be certain that the unions were established on the non-political model that it desired. The conflict between past policies on African labour and the new direction being pursued by the Colonial Office came to a head in 1940 when, after white miners had gone on strike and won substantial pay increases, African miners also went on strike for higher pay. As in 1935, the strikers were met by force. Yet the Forster Commission of Inquiry, set up after the strike, recommended a pay increase for African workers, and made some observations on the desirability of letting African workers advance into European categories of employment.

The return of white miners at the end of the war halted even the small experiments in African advancement that had occurred during the war years. But, with the growing organisation of African workers into trade unions, accompanied by pressure from the Colonial Office, and the interest of mining employers in replacing expatriate workers by less expensive Africans, African advancement became an increasingly important issue in labour relations in Zambia. By virtue of the African miners' improved bargaining position, and the investment in 'stabilisation' that the mining companies wanted to protect, African wages rose rapidly after 1940. However, higher wages after 1940 did not diminish African workers' desire to move up to even better paid jobs. In response to pressures on this account, the 1947 Dalgleish Commission was appointed to inquire specifically into African advancement, and made some very moderate recommendations towards its implementation. But even these proved too extreme for the unions representing white workers, who stood firm in their insistence upon 'equal pay for equal work and responsibility', otherwise known as 'the rate for the job', a principle which, if accepted, removed any economic incentive for the mining companies to advance Africans into European categories of employment. The European mineworkers' union made it clear that its members would accept African advancement only on condition that African workers were appointed at European rates of pay.

Against this background, the Guillebaud Tribunal of 1953, arbitrating in a dispute between the mining companies and the African mineworkers' union felt

> bound to place on record [its] profound conviction that satisfactory and harmonious industrial relations on the Copperbelt will not be attained unless or until effective steps have been taken to enable the African workers to advance to positions of greater responsibility and importance than those which are now open to them.[1]

The Northern Rhodesian Government responded by appointing a second Commission of Inquiry to investigate African advancement, the 1954 Forster Commission. This commission accepted the need for the Africanisation and 'reasonable fragmentation'[2] of a number of jobs hitherto reserved for Europeans. It recommended that the rates of pay for fragmented jobs should not necessarily be based upon the former European scales. Predictably, the European union would not accept the proposals, but, in the wake of the collapse of the Korean War commodities boom, the economic pressures on the mining companies to implement a programme of African advancement increased, while the bargaining strength of the European mineworkers diminished.

As copper prices, and copper mining profits, fell in 1953 and 1954, the potential gains in profits from replacing expatriates by lower-paid African workers came to look increasingly attractive when compared with the falling level of profits earned by the mines. At the same time, the falling profits meant that a strike by white miners brought with it the risk that mines might have to be closed down and some of the strikers would be thrown out of employment. Thus when, in 1955, the Rhodesian Selection Trust mining group terminated its recognition agreement with the European mineworkers' union, with a view to advancing Africans into some of the jobs covered by the old agreement, there was relatively little hostile reaction from the white union. A new recognition agreement was negotiated releasing a few former European jobs for Africanisation, but 'the rate for the job' was maintained in all other European jobs. Some further jobs were taken out of the European scale and Africanised in 1960.

The mining companies, of course, had anticipated the prospect of African advancement, and were concerned to prevent the movement of some Africans into better-paid employment from pulling up African wage scales generally. In part, they achieved this by paying the newly promoted Africans at lower rates than those paid to Europeans in the same jobs. But of possibly greater significance was the mines' encouragement of the establishment, in 1953, of the Mines African Staff Association, to act as a union for the most senior African mineworkers. The Staff Association covered those categories of employment involved in African advancement, and therefore the negotiation of wages for the bulk of African mineworkers (represented by the NRAMU) was kept virtually separate from that for the mineworkers affected by Africanisation.

At the end of this first era, at the start of 1961, wages in most sectors in Zambia were decided in a similar manner to the dominant mining sector. At the top of the pay scale were the European workers, protected by their powerful unions, and whose earnings were fixed in a fairly stable relationship to those for similar workers outside Zambia. Then came the small number of Africans who had benefited from the first moves towards African advancement. In some sectors, such as government administration, these workers were employed on similar terms to their European counterparts, but in others, like the mines, the beneficiaries from Africanisation received incomes well below those received by non-Africans in similar jobs. Beneath them one found the bulk of the African wage labour force, unskilled or semiskilled workers with little prospect of moving into skilled employment, whose real wages had risen significantly since 1930 by virtue of the employers' interest in minimising labour turnover and in preventing labour unrest. However, despite these workers' gains from unionisation and collective bargaining, their wages remained well below those earned by their colleagues moving into former European jobs.

Towards a Unified Pay Scale: 1961 to 1967

The first acceptance by major employment sectors of the principle of African advancement into the full range of jobs occupied by Europeans occurred in 1961. In that year, Rhodesia Railways opened its European categories of employment to Africans, although 'the rate for the job' remained the rule. In November of the same year, the European and African Civil Services were combined into a non-racial Northern Rhodesia Civil Services (Local Conditions) but nothing was done to bring the wages for the former European and African jobs into one common scale.

The 1962 Morison Commission of Inquiry, considering the mining industry's pay structure, attempted to resolve the conflict that had arisen between the mining companies and the Northern Rhodesia African Mineworkers' Union, representing the lower-paid African mineworkers, over the way in which African advancement was to be related to the creation of a single, unified non-racial pay scale throughout the mining industry. The Morison Commission pinpointed the nature of this disagreement when it observed that

> Throughout our hearings, there has been apparent a difference between what 'African advancement' means to the companies and to the African Union. The companies lay their emphasis on providing a ladder which more Africans will climb as more become qualified. The African Union says that these at most will be a favoured few, and sees African advancement as consisting chiefly in lifting the great majority of its members, who are in the lower ticket paid groups, nearer to Schedule 'A'.[3]

In its eventual recommendations, the Morison Commission proposed a compromise, raising African wages by a constant proportion throughout the scale, but not entirely closing the gap between the African and European pay scales.

It was only in 1964, however, the year after the attainment of self-government, that a major employment sector created a truly uniform, non-racial wage and employment structure. This turning point occurred with the report of the Hadow Salaries Commission which reviewed the salaries of the Civil Service. The Hadow Commission had been faced with four separate pay scales within the Civil Service, differing according to the race or the date of employment of the civil servant. The commission proposed the creation of one single scale to cover all civil servants. Lower-paid civil servants were awarded a sizable pay increase, but the commission recommended reducing salaries for the entire range of former 'European' jobs, feeling that, having taken account of the 'requirements of the local employment market', a pay increase for more senior workers 'would mean paying many local African officers more than their market value requires and would be unacceptable on financial grounds'.[4]

While the period following the collapse of the Federation of Rhodesia and Nyasaland was generally associated with an improvement in working conditions for African wage workers, European employees felt increasingly unsettled. On Rhodesia Railways, and on the copper mines, labour unrest among expatriates was considerable during 1964. In those sectors, as well as in central and local government, the rate of turnover of expatriate staff reached unprecedented levels. Some idea of the increasing stability of the African work force and growing instability of European workers in the mining industry can be gathered from the figures given in Table 5.2, page 106. With employers concerned to stem the loss of skilled workers, expatriates secured sizable increases in pay and special allowances (variously called contract, inducement or expatriate allowances) although as Table 5.2 reveals, these had little effect in reducing expatriate turnover.

It was against the background of awards similar to that of the 1964 Hadow Commission on public sector salaries, which created one unified pay scale in which expatriate employees received a uniform pattern of expatriate allowances, that the mines moved back towards an anachronistic dualistic wage structure. The labour movement in the mining sector in 1964 was rent by a struggle between the longer established Northern Rhodesia African Mineworkers' Union (NRAMU) and the new United Mineworkers' Union (UMU),[5] created out of the former

Table 5.2: Labour Turnover on the Copper Mines (as Percentage of Labour Force Leaving Employment per Month)

Year	Africans	Europeans
1959	2.5	1.4
1960	2.5	1.4
1961	1.9	1.8
1962	1.4	1.3
1963	0.8	2.8
1964	0.7	2.1
1965	0.6	1.8
1966	0.6	2.6
1967	0.5	2.4
1968	0.5	2.5
1969	0.5	2.3
1970	0.4	2.2
1971	0.7	1.9
1972	0.7	2.1
1973	0.6	2.2
1974	0.7	2.0
1975	0.8	2.3
1976	0.6	2.7

Sources: *Department of Labour Annual Reports* (1960-72); *Zambia Mining Year-book* (1976).

Mines African Staff Association (MASA) as a result of an attempt backed by the United National Independence Party (UNIP) to secure control of organised African mineworkers. In the course of the struggle the mines withdrew official recognition from the UMU, effectively leaving the higher-paid Africans, in the staff grades formerly covered by the MASA, without any recognised negotiating representative. The threat from the UMU increased the pressure upon the leadership of the NRAMU to secure a pay increase for lower-paid mineworkers, to emphasise its effectiveness to its members. Thus, when the mining companies put forward proposals to increase wages at the bottom of the scale, while decreasing the wages of Africans advanced into former European jobs, the miners adversely affected by such an agreement were powerless to prevent the proposals from being implemented.

The effect of the 1964 mining pay award was to create two entirely separate, expatriate and local pay scales, without any recognisable rationale to explain the considerable variation in the differentials between the two scales. Once the UMU, at the end of 1964, ceased its attempts to displace the NRAMU, and reformed itself into the Mines Local Staff Association, the predictable opposition to the 1964 agreement materialised. The crisis atmosphere following the Rhodesian UDI and wrangling over the form of constitution of the mineworkers' union (then named the Zambia Mineworkers' Union) prevented matters from coming to a head in 1965. Eventually, however, even the granting of a uniform 8 per cent wage award to African miners in January 1966 could not prevent dissatisfaction over racial pay disparities from erupting into outright strike action.

The Zambian Government responded by appointing a Commission of Inquiry under the chairmanship of Roland Brown, with instructions to examine the disparities between the expatriate and local conditions of service. In its report, the commission recommended establishing a single basic pay scale, with expatriate allowances for foreign workers. However, the commission faced considerable difficulty in deciding what factors should determine the basic pay scale. The existing expatriate pay scale was rejected as a basis because (a) it would be excessively inflationary, (b) it was based on an inappropriate notion of privilege, being fixed sufficiently high to secure a 'European way of life' for those on that pay scale, and (c) because the effect of collective bargaining in the past had been to introduce widespread anomalies into the scale.[6] The former local scale was also unacceptable as a basis because

> it deliberately undervalues the skill of African workers. It has been built from established points on the scale of African wages by a process of job evaluation, without reference to European rates for the same or similar work. The European miners were able to secure for themselves high wages because industrial skill in Zambia was scarce. It is still scarce and will remain so for many years to come. Its value to the employer does not depend on race or colour, but by isolating African wages from any connection with European wages the mining companies appear . . . to have devalued the skill which Africans can acquire now for the first time.[7]

The Brown Commission eventually recommended a 22 per cent wage increase to be applied uniformly throughout the former African scale, but the choice of the figure of 22 per cent was clearly arbitrary. The selection of such a high rate of increase was undoubtedly influenced less by any scientific calculations of the 'correct' relationship of the new to the old pay scales than by the commission's belief that the mines found themselves in

> a situation which must be put right if there is to be any chance of industrial peace. Weighing in the balance the importance of the industry on which the development of Zambia ultimately depends, we have felt justified in recommending, as part of a new settlement, a general increase in wages which might otherwise be regarded as excessive in terms of the growth rate of the economy as a whole.[8]

The Brown Commission Report was very quickly followed by that of the Whelan Civil Service Salaries Commission, appointed shortly after the appointment of the Brown Commission. The Whelan Commission was not concerned with combining two separate, expatriate and local pay scales. Instead it was asked particularly to take account of wage awards in other fields and to tackle the disparity between lower and higher civil service salaries.

The Whelan Commission eventually proposed wage awards which increased average salaries of civil servants by something like the 22 per cent selected by the Brown Commission. But the Whelan Commission differed considerably from the Brown Commission in tapering its awards so that workers earning less than £500 a year would receive at least a 25 per cent increase and workers in the £500 to £1,000 range would receive 20 per cent, while 15 per cent was recommended for those on higher incomes. The Whelan Commission also proposed ending the differentials between rural and urban civil services pay scale, thereby virtually doubling the pay of the lowest-paid rural civil servants. Following the Whelan award, statutory minimum wages were increased in all sectors by the 20 to 25 per cent level established as a precedent by the Brown and the Whelan Commission awards. Most sectors followed the example of the Whelan Commission in ending rural/urban pay differentials, and the general minimum wage in rural areas doubled from 7½d to 1s 3d per hour.

Thus the second of our three eras of wage determination can be seen to have ended with the attainment of a unified wage scale in all major employment sectors. Outside the mines, the changeover to one basic pay scale was achieved without much difficulty. But the problems of the mining unions in 1964 caused the changeover in the mining sector to be delayed until 1966. In some sectors, as the Whelan Commission findings illustrate, wage awards took account of wage differentials within the basic pay scale, and reduced the size of the earnings gap between workers at the top and the bottom of the scale. There can be little doubt, however, that the average rate of pay increase in all sectors between 1961 and 1967 owed more to the unification of the pay scales in the mining sector than to any other factor.

The Era of Incomes Policy 1967-74

The round of wage increases averaging over 20 per cent, and sparked off by the Brown Commission award, continued for much of 1967. But in August of that year came the first sign of official concern over the pace of wage increases. The National Joint Council for Local Authority workers agreed upon an award, raising the minimum wage of the lowest-paid local government employees from K27 to K32 per month, only to discover that the Ministry of Local Government and Housing refused to sanction any increase above K28.17. The ministry remained firm in the face of strike action, and local government minimum wages did not reach K32 until 1970.

Local government workers were unfortunate to have been the last in line for the 1966-7 wage awards, and the first group to have been penalised as part of a stricter policy on pay increases. Industrial relations among other major groups of wage workers were much improved following their wage awards. The ZMU merged with the unions representing the African mines staff and mine policemen in 1967 to form the Mineworkers' Union of Zambia (MUZ), which became the sole union in the mining industry. After two years of negotiations, the MUZ and the mining companies in early 1969 reached agreement on a joint job evaluation scheme to create a new grading structure.

With the mines preparing the ground for their next pay award, the government in March 1969 announced the establishment of a Salaries Commission to review Civil Service salaries. In the meantime, however, during the latter part of 1969, an official incomes policy started to emerge, in time, it was clearly hoped, to anticipate and restrain the next round of large wage increases. Professor H.A. Turner arrived in Zambia in August 1969, to prepare his report on such a policy, and in the same month, President Kaunda ordered a temporary wage freeze and a ban on unofficial strikes. In his report, Professor Turner blamed higher wages without correspondingly higher labour productivity for Zambia's unprecedented rate of inflation after 1966 and for the marked slowdown in employment creation. Consequently the Second National Convention in December 1969 was sympathetic to Turner's condemnation of the low productivity of Zambian workers and his call for a system of wage and price controls. And it was in this spirit that the convention approved Dr Kaunda's announcement, made at the convention, that wage increases would henceforth be limited to 5 per cent per annum.

From the government's point of view, the policy was announced only just in time, since the first important wage award since 1967, a flat K8 per month increase for all railway workers, was just about to be implemented. In respect of lower-paid workers, the award violated the limit on pay awards. The Ministry of Power, Transport and Works therefore intervened to reduce the award. After strike action, a compromise was reached to divide the award into two annual increases of K4.00 and remain within the policy guidelines.

The railway workers' strike was not the only one of 1970. There was also a series of unofficial strikes by school teachers in protest against the delay in the implementation of new conditions of service. Although the leaders of the Zambia National Union of Teachers (ZNUT), in line with government policy, issued a condemnation of the striking school teachers, the government clearly doubted the sincerity of the condemnation and placed several ZNUT leaders in detention. In 1966, the government had detained a leader of the expatriate mineworkers' union, in order to end a strike by expatriate mineworkers, but the action against the ZNUT leaders was much harsher than anything ever attempted previously to control the Zambian trade union movement. In its immediate objective of ending the teachers' strike, the detentions proved very effective.

Despite the unrest elsewhere, the 1970 mines pay award, signed in September, was agreed without strike action having occurred. Since the award was the result of a complex grading exercise, the award varied from job to job, but the average increase was of the order of 10 per cent. Some workers, however, were downgraded in the agreement[9] and received no pay rise at all. As in 1964 and January 1966, the imminence of MUZ elections in September 1970 may have persuaded the MUZ leadership to accept such a moderate pay rise. For later that month, MUZ branch elections were held, and in the initial satisfaction with the new award, with workers receiving backdated wage increments in their pay packets, most of the incumbent union officials were returned to office.

But discontent with the award could not be concealed for long, and surfaced during the November 1970 elections for MUZ head office officials, which were characterised by sharp disagreement between the former executive and its critics who came increasingly to be associated with opposition to the new grading system. The government, ever alert to the political repercussions of conflict within the trade union movement, intervened to defuse the issue to the benefit of the former executive by appointing Abel Musonda, who had opposed the incumbent, David Mwila, in the election for the presidency of the MUZ, to a District Governor's post away from the Copperbelt. At the same time, the forces favouring increased centralisation of the trade union movement gained in strength from the co-option of Wilson Chakulya, General Secretary of the Zambia Congress of Trade Unions, into the Cabinet, where he soon became Minister of Labour and Social Services.

Despite government intervention, opposition to the 1970 award persisted, particularly among the mines staff grades, who, with memories possibly of their downgrading in 1964, were resentful at having to suffer a disproportionate share of the downgrading which occurred in 1970. In May 1971, notices appeared in several mine townships calling for unofficial strike action. The government reacted firmly, as it had done earlier with the teachers, and before any strikes could occur, arrested 100 dissident miners and later detained 15 of their leaders.

May 1971 also saw the presentation of the Government's response to the O'Riordan Salaries Commission Report on Public Service salaries,[10] which had been given a number of interesting terms of reference. These included restricting pay increases within the 5 per cent incomes policy limit; the need to attract people to work in rural areas; the modification of the system of housing subsidies; consideration of Zambian wages in relation to those of neighbouring friendly states; and the need to establish some relationship between civil service and parastatal salary scales.

Considering the potential scope for innovation given by these terms of reference, the O'Riordan Commission's Report was disappointing. On wages, for example, the commission recommended wage increases averaging 15 to 20 per cent, within the incomes policy norm, but chose to exceed the norm when fixing wage levels for the highest paid civil servants. The government defended this on the grounds that the increases amounted to less than 5 per cent per annum in disposable incomes, after allowing for the impact of progressive income tax and higher house rentals. Thus the government was content deliberately to counteract the progressive, redistributional nature of the income tax system, and to use the incomes policy to maintain differentials in disposable incomes—altogether a remarkably non-egalitarian view of incomes policy.

As regards housing subsidies, the commission recommended removing the ceiling that formerly existed on civil service rents, and wanted to move eventually to a system of economic rentals, though, in the event, nothing was done to achieve the latter objective. Despite the terms of reference, no mention whatever was made of wage levels in neighbouring states in the published report. But the commission did recommend action to bring conditions in parastatals and local government into line with those in central government. Again, however, no action was taken to implement this recommendation.

The government's and commission's views on attracting civil servants to rural areas were scarcely less disappointing than their views on the other terms of reference. For, while a system of national prices for basic commodities was recommended for further consideration as a means of bringing rural and urban costs of living more into line with one another, the government went on to note that, while it felt

> some sympathy for public servants serving in rural areas, their position is no more difficult than that of the general populace in those areas. The commission's view that public servants should be required to work at any station in Zambia without compensation for the situation existing at that station is appreciated.[11]

As in 1966/7, most statutory minimum wages were raised in the wake of the copper mining and central government awards. The rises approved by the Ministry of Labour and Social Services varied between 12 per cent for the 'better off' building, civil engineering and motor workers and 27 per cent for agricultural labourers.

Again reflecting events of five years earlier, the two years after 1971 were quiet as regards pay negotiations and labour disputes. But in late 1973 the next wage round started. And as had so consistently been the case before, the mines award, granting increases averaging 20 per cent, came first in late 1973, and was announced only a few months before the four-yearly MUZ branch elections were held. The pattern of the years since independence was also repeated, in that most of the former officers were returned in the elections. Nevertheless, there was a strong challenge to the old leadership from the dissident elements which had emerged in 1970 and 1971. At Mufulira some of the candidates standing against incumbent officers were arrested several days before the branch election, thereby marking a further stage in the governmental involvement in trade union affairs. Despite such intimidation, several leading dissidents secured election to important branch posts from which they could embarrass the head office leadership. However, when the elections for head office posts were held later in the year, the anticipated dissident challenge failed to materialise.

A new Government Salaries Commission, chaired by John Mwanakatwe, former Minister of Finance, was not appointed until August 1974, and its report was published one year later.[12] The terms of reference that it was presented with were similar to those of its immediate predecessor, but the two commissions' recommendations differed considerably. On wages, the Mwanakatwe Commission proposed a tapering set of awards, ranging from nearly 40 per cent at the bottom of the scale to 5 per cent at the top – though the government later reduced this latter to one of only 2 per cent. Changes proposed in fringe benefits, such as a lowering of house rentals, ran counter to the spirit of the O'Riordan Commission, and had the effect of raising disposable incomes by an extra 5 per cent or so over and above the basic award, but these alterations too were tapered so as to benefit low-paid workers relatively more than the well paid. One particular innovation in the Mwanakatwe report was the use of a Poverty Datum Line estimate of K40 per month as the basis for its lowest wage awards.

The O'Riordan and Mwanakatwe Commissions concurred when they came to make proposals on rural allowances and the relationship between parastatal and Civil Service conditions of service. To the Mwanakatwe Commission a rural areas allowance was unacceptable, since it would 'create a new class of Zambians serving as expatriates in their own country'.[13] And, like the O'Riordan report, it was firmly in favour of bringing parastatal and Civil Service pay scales into line with one another. The commission's preference was for a 5 per cent pay advantage for parastatal workers to reflect the more 'onerous' working conditions and lower job security in parastatal employment,[14] but the government rejected any premium for parastatal employees.

The Mwanakatwe awards were more generous than the 1973 mining agreement, and were made public after a period of petty labour troubles on the Copperbelt. Hence the government was concerned lest the 1975 public sector pay increases would cause resentment among mineworkers. It was presumably to forestall any such trouble that, at the same time as the Mwanakatwe awards were published, the Minister of Mines and Industry announced the granting of pay rises for copper miners, ranging from 20 per cent for the lowest paid to 7 per cent at the top of the scale – thereby preserving the pre-1973 sectoral wage differentials. But unlike the experience in most previous wage rounds, the miners had barely a year to wait before they received their next pay award. As the wage round percolated through the economy during the course of 1976, the copper mines negotiated a new three year pay agreement with the MUZ, granting pay rises similar to those awarded in 1975. Thus mineworkers entered 1978 relatively better paid (in comparison with other major employment sectors) than they had been since the attainment of independence.

Summary

The present chapter's brief historical survey of wage determination has described the dominant role played by the copper mines as a wage leader in the Zambian economy. Typically, the copper miners' pay award sets the pattern of all subsequent agreements. However, the experience of the past three years indicates that, if inflation appears to be eroding the miners' position substantially, then action is taken to ensure that they do not suffer relative to other important groups of workers.

In Chapter 6 the author analyses the determinants of wages as they relate to the four differentials mentioned at the start of this chapter. Sectoral differentials are, of course, an important aspect of this, but we shall see that changes in the differentials within sectors are equally significant in the context of the present study.

Notes

1. *Report and Award of the Arbitrator C.W. Guillebaud Esq., C.B.E., nominated under the Industrial Conciliation Ordinance to arbitrate in a Dispute between the Northern Rhodesia African Mineworkers' Trade Union and the Copper Mining Companies* (Kitwe, January 1953), p. 13, para. 28.

2. 'Job fragmentation' occurs when the work formerly performed by one worker is divided so that the work is now undertaken by a large number of workers. Each new worker therefore performs only a fragment of the work performed by a worker in the former situation. In this way semi-skilled workers can replace workers who possess greater skills.

3. *Report of the Commission Appointed to Inquire into the Mining Industry in Northern Rhodesia* (Government Printer, Lusaka, 1962), para. 52. Note that lower-paid miners were paid according to 'tickets' of 30 shifts. Schedule 'A' consisted of those jobs still reserved for European miners.

4. *Report of the Commission Appointed to Review the Salaries and Conditions of Service of the Northern Rhodesia Public and Teaching Services, and of the Northern Rhodesia Army and Air Force* (Hadow Commission Report) (Government Printer, Lusaka, 1964), paras. 60-70.

5. Accounts of the struggle between the ruling United National Independence Party and the trade union movement for control of the unions representing mineworkers are given in K. Quinn, 'Industrial Relations in Zambia: 1935-1969', in C. Elliott (ed.), *Constraints on the Economic Development of Zambia* (Oxford University Press, Nairobi, 1971), and R.H. Bates, *Unions, Parties and Political Development: A Study of Mineworkers in Zambia* (Yale University Press, New Haven, 1971).

6. *Report of the Commission of Inquiry into the Mining Industry* (Brown

Commission Report) (Government Printer, Lusaka, 1966), para. 112.

7. Brown Commission Report, para. 114.

8. Brown Commission Report, para. 117. The members of the commission only expected their award to bring 2 years of industrial peace. (See C. Harvey, 'Control of Inflation in a very open Economy – Zambia, 1964-1969', in *Eastern African Economic Review*, vol. 3.1, June 1971, fn. 19, p. 60.) In fact it was 5 years before signs of industrial unrest re-emerged among copper miners.

9. The number downgraded was estimated at 1,000 by David Mwila, President of the MUZ, in the *Zambia Daily Mail*, 14 October 1971.

10. The original report was never published.

11. Government Report No. 1 of 1971, *Report of the Commission Appointed to Review the Salaries, Salary Structure and Conditions of Service of the Zambia Public Service* (O'Riordan Commission Report) (Government Printer, Lusaka, May 1971), p. 9, para. 23.

12. *Report of the Commission of Inquiry into the Salaries, Salary Structure and Conditions of Service, Volume One, The Public Services and the Parastatal Sector* (Mwanakatwe Commission Report) (Government Printer, Lusaka, 1975).

13. *Report of Commission of Inquiry into Salaries, Salary Structure and Conditions of Service*, para. 10.193, p. 107.

14. *Report of Commission of Inquiry into Salaries, Salary Structure and Conditions of Service*, para. 14.6, p. 146.

6 ISSUES IN WAGE DETERMINATION–THE FOUR MAIN DIFFERENTIALS

As indicated in Chapter 5, our analysis of the main issues affecting wage determination is to be presented in terms of four differentials within the structure of incomes in Zambia. These differentials, to which we now turn, are (i) the expatriate/local wage differential, (ii) the rural/urban income differential, (iii) sectoral earnings differentials, and (iv) the skilled/unskilled differential.

The Expatriate/Local Wage Differential

Differences between local and expatriate conditions of service can be seen to have had a very strong influence on the determination of wage scales throughout the period before 1967. The powerful expatriate Northern Rhodesia Mineworkers' Union (NRMWU) used its bargaining position as the sole supplier of skilled labour to the copper mines not only to force expatriate earnings above earnings for comparable jobs in countries such as South Africa or Southern Rhodesia, but also, until 1955, successfully to preserve their areas of employment as expatriate-only domains. Furthermore, the expatriates succeeded, through their elected members on the Legislative Council, in entrenching their privileged position more firmly than would have been possible on the basis of collective bargaining alone. For example, until 1959 Africans were forbidden by law from becoming apprenticed, and were thereby automatically ineligible for a wide range of skilled employment; secondary and higher educational opportunities for Europeans were vastly better than those for Africans; and health, housing, land ownership, social and other facilities were reserved for Europeans.

It was inevitable in the circumstances that the question of African advancement and the related issue of the appropriate differentials, if any, between the African and expatriate pay scales should, for so long, have been one of the major problems in wage determination. Although the question first arose in 1940, the mining companies, torn between the expatriates' intransigent opposition to African advancement and their own (and the Colonial Office's) desires for African advancement, were happy to buy peace during a period of steadily rising copper prices and growing mining profits by granting pay rises to African miners to narrow somewhat the expatriate/African earnings differential.

When copper prices fell after 1953, the economic interest of the copper mines shifted. No longer was it an attractive policy to buy peace with higher wages. Instead, the mines saw greater advantages in risking confrontation with the NRMWU and lowering production costs through the replacement of expatriates by Africans. Furthermore, European miners were less prepared to take strike action during a period of low mining profits for fear of jeopardising their own careers and the future of their mines. Thus African advancement at last became a real possibility, and was implemented partially in 1955.

Through their tactic of divide and rule, by means of the creation of separate unions for African staff and lower-grade African miners, the mines hoped to insulate the wage scales of the bulk of unskilled African mineworkers from the influence of the European scales into which a small number of African staff were advancing. But this tactic could succeed only for a short while, and by 1961 it was evident that each sector would have to introduce a unified non-racial pay structure for local workers, supplemented by special allowances for expatriates recruited from abroad. Merely to open former European jobs to Africans was not acceptable to most workers, as the comments of the Morison Commission quoted in Chapter 5 make clear; and to move towards two entirely separate wage structures for European and African workers, as the mines did in 1964, was even less acceptable.

The demands for the unification of the pay scale and the establishment of a consistent set of expatriate allowances thus came to overshadow all other issues in wage negotiation in the dominant mining sector, and were satisfied only after the 1966 report of the Brown Commission. Since that date, the issue of the differences between the expatriate and local pay scales has ceased to exert any noticeable influence on Zambian wage bargaining. With the steady decline in the proportion of expatriates in the labour force, there is little prospect that the issue will ever again impinge strongly on local wage determination.

Since independence in 1964, the issue that has come to overshadow that of expatriate/local wage differentials has been the related one of Zambianisation. As Burawoy's paper[1] describes so well, Zambianisation creates a variety of tensions within the labour force. Besides the obvious tension between an expatriate and his successor, there will be conflicting claims for the successor's post originating, on the one hand, from the older, more experienced Zambian, likely to be preferred by conservative expatriates, and, on the other, from the younger, better educated generation of recent secondary school leavers and university graduates.

Another source of frustration gives rise to the paradoxical situation described, but not analysed fully, by Burawoy, whereby the present pace of Zambianisation is criticised at one and the same time for being too slow and yet for causing substantial inefficiency. In fact the paradox is more apparent than real, since the long-run benefits from Zambianisation can hardly fail to be accompanied by some short-run disruptions during the stage of transition to Zambian staffing of senior positions. There remains, however, one instance where the official policy towards Zambianisation has followed contradictory courses of action. This is in its approach to technical as opposed to white-collar posts.

While the Zambianisation of white-collar positions, first of all in the Civil Service, but, by the late 1960s, in all sectors, has been encouraged as forcefully as possible, the Zambianisation of technical positions has been allowed to lag, so much so that one might take the neglect to be a deliberate part of government policy. As a reaction against the colonial, racially biased system of technical training, the newly independent Zambian Government abandoned the system of formal technical education inherited from the federal era, and virtually ignored the field until 1969, when Valentine Musakanya built up the Commission for Technical Education and Vocational Training with proselytising zeal. The bias against technical education was entrenched even at university level. Despite their paramount importance in the national economy, two of the last Schools established at the University of Zambia were those of Agriculture and Mines. Indeed, pressure from the mining companies, rather than from the central government, was responsible for the School of Mines opening as early as it did, in 1972, six years after Schools such as Humanities and Social Science.

The relative neglect of the Zambianisation of technical posts makes the effective Zambianisation of the remainder of the economy harder to achieve. Zambians are filling an ever increasing proportion of administrative, decision making posts, while the technical analysis that so often pre-empts administrators' decisions comes from expatriates, and is likely to have to come from them for a long time to come. In a later section of this chapter on 'The Skilled/Unskilled Differential' we shall return to a comparison of the conditions of technical and administrative employment.

The Rural/Urban Income Differential

The expatriate/local wage differential, although an important determinant of the local Zambian wage scale, can be identified as having exerted a major influence on wage levels only for the two decades before 1967.

The difference between expatriate and local wages does not adequately explain the trend in African wage rates either before the early 1940s or after the mid-1960s. Abstracting, for the time being, from the factors which may determine the differentials within the wage structure across sectors and across occupations, we need to find something other than expatriates' wages to explain how local wages have moved.

One popular alternative explanation of the determination of local wages would be in terms of a clearly defined relationship with the private opportunity cost of workers giving up self-employment in the traditional sector to enter wage employment (the more neoclassical approach), or with the cost of reproducing labour power – namely the value of subsistence earnings (the more classical approach). In other words, one might expect to find some consistent relationship between urban wages and the marginal product of agricultural labour, or between urban wages and the imputed value of subsistence agricultural production.

Prior to the early 1940s, the classical, Marxist analysis appears to hold true. During that period, Arrighi's comments on the Southern Rhodesian situation hold with equal force for Northern Rhodesia: 'real wages remained at a level which promoted capitalist accumulation not because of the forces of supply and demand, but because of politico-economic mechanisms that ensured the "desired" supply at the "desired wage rate".'[2] The combination of poll taxation payable only in cash and controls on African agriculture meant that employers found it possible to recruit workers even though the wages that they offered were, in real terms, very similar to subsistence earnings.

Nevertheless, as mentioned previously, some employers found it to be to their own advantage if they provided their unskilled African workers with more than mere subsistence rations. On the mines, for example, during the early 1930s, employers found it very profitable to emulate their counterparts at Union Minière in Katanga and stabilise their labour force by raising the real standards of living that they provided for their employees.[3] They soon discovered that, once they had improved their workers' physical condition and reduced labour turnover, remarkable gains in labour efficiency could be achieved from treating the labour force as a heterogeneous group that would benefit from training in a variety of semi-skilled occupations.

But the gains from stabilisation, while providing a good reason why urban wage levels would be expected to lie some way above rural subsistence earnings, are insufficient to explain why, since 1966, wages, particularly at the bottom of the scale, and in the lower paying sectors, such as agriculture or rural local government, should have moved so far above the subsistence level and so far above incomes in traditional agriculture. To explain this, we have to look outside 'pure' economics and examine the other factors affecting wage determination at the present moment. For our purposes, the best way to appreciate the impact of these other factors is to consider wage determination as a quadripartite process involving the employers, the unions, the workers and the government.

It might be supposed that the unions and workers always want increased pay, while the employers and government (itself a very large employer) want to restrict pay increases. However, in the case of Zambia such an analysis would be extremely simplistic. If we deal with the employers first, while their interest is to increase profits, it is not always evident that they consider wage control to be an important way in which to increase profits. For one thing, the possibilities of substituting capital for labour may be so great that higher labour costs are virtually offset by increasing the degree of mechanisation of production. Another reason for suspecting that there will be low resistance from the mining companies, at any rate, to wage increases for their workers is that in mining, as in some of the more important sectors, labour costs are only a small proportion of the value of gross output. African wages for example, accounted directly for only 10.25 per cent of the value of copper mining output in 1967. In these circumstances, the concession of a few percentage points of wage increases to workers has only a small effect on profits, and may even appear less costly than the loss of profits if strikes occur. A one-week strike on the copper mines costs much more in lost profits than the annual cost of a 10 per cent pay award for African miners.

Yet the copper mines are likely to be more stubborn than many other sectors in the face of demands for higher pay. For the copper mines are one of the very few sectors which face world market prices over which they have little control. Most other sectors in Zambia cater for the domestic market, in which it is usual to pass higher labour costs on to the customer via higher selling prices. Even where competition from imports might be supposed to restrict local firms' ability to push up prices, requests for greater tariff protection or tightness in the issue of import licences greatly reduce the realisation of the potential of such competition. There are yet other sectors which do not sell their product at all – the government itself is the biggest example – and the concern for profits clearly does not influence wage determination in them. Finally, there are sectors other than copper mining, which sell a share of their output on world markets – lead and zinc mining, or tobacco and maize farming – to which the government has shown itself willing to pay subsidies (via tax concessions or guaranteed producer prices) to protect them from the adverse effects of high labour costs.

If we add to the picture the oft-cited desire of foreign companies to improve their public image by being seen to be kind and generous employers, then it is evident that the pressure from the employers' side for wage restraint is not as strong as might generally be believed.

The interest of the government is not so clearcut either. From the purely economic point of view, wage control is well in line with government objectives, since lower wages are likely to assist in the attainment of higher employment, lower rates of inflation, a greater inflow of foreign investment and higher government revenue (derived from high company profits). Yet in Zambia, as elsewhere, political considerations count for a great deal in determining official policy on wage determination. And in wage determination in Zambia, the government's political considerations appear to be very specifically concerned with achieving control over the activities of the trade union movement, and over the Mineworkers' Union of Zambia (MUZ), in particular.

In our historical review of wage determination in Zambia (Chapter 5), we described how, from its very inception, the trade union movement was independent of the African nationalist movement. Indeed, it was to create such independence that the colonial authorities actively encouraged the formation of African trade unions during the late 1940s, before the mass African nationalist movement had become established. Epstein, Quinn and Bates[4] have all testified to the success of the Colonial Office's strategy. The main African mineworkers' union remained outside the political manoeuvres that led up to the eventual attainment of political independence, and the union consistently refused to get involved in the attempts to use strikes to further the nationalist cause. That the mineworkers remained aloof from the nationalist movement was in no way owing to their lack of support for, first, the African National Congress (ANC) and, after its split, for the United National Independence Party (UNIP). With the exception of Mufulira, the Copperbelt remained a UNIP stronghold, and several miners' leaders became leaders of UNIP. Yet the miners remained careful to keep their trade union affairs separate from party politics.

UNIP became extremely suspicious of the trade union movement, seeing it not only as a possible obstacle in the implementation of an incomes policy, but also, possibly even more important, seeing in it the potential threat of a large, well organised political force, with financial resources of its own, and a fairly homogeneous, unified and geographically concentrated membership. If the control of the MUZ or the Zambia Congress of Trade Unions (ZCTU) moved into the hands of interests hostile to UNIP, the political consequences could be very serious indeed. Therefore, UNIP has chosen to pursue a two-pronged strategy in dealing with organised labour. On the one hand, UNIP has attempted to secure control over the trade union movement. The formation of the United Mineworkers' Union in 1963 and its struggle to oust the Northern Rhodesia African Mineworkers' Union was an (unsuccessful) example of this strategy. Trade union leaders were also co-opted into parliament, into the Cabinet (during the 1970s, two General Secretaries of the ZCTU, Wilson Chakulya and Basil Kabwe, have been co-opted in this way), or were appointed directors of government-controlled companies, and received the fringe benefits associated with these posts. Those leaders whom the government found troublesome were appointed to posts outside the union movement or, as with the teachers' union officers or dissident mineworkers' officials, were placed in detention.

The formation in 1971, by the former Vice-President, Simon Kapwepwe, of a new opposition party, the United Progressive Party (UPP), the involvement of (and subsequent detention of) a number of trade union officials in the affairs of the UPP, and the election of Kapwepwe to Parliament to represent a Mufulira seat, all served to confirm in the minds of many UNIP activists the need to secure greater control over the trade union movement. This was reflected in part in a push towards the centralisation of the Zambia Congress of Trade Unions, and the encouragement of the creation of UNIP branches at places of work. But there was also an increase in direct government intervention in the affairs of individual unions, exemplified by the arrest of a number of candidates for MUZ branch elections in Mufulira in 1974.

However, the UNIP Government tactics did not consist solely of wielding a big stick to force the unions into submission. There was undoubtedly also an extent to which official policy was to dangle attractive carrots before union members, and support them in their demands for higher pay. Thus, in 1966, UNIP intervened on behalf of the mineworkers during the presentation of evidence to the Brown Commission and charged the mines with 'putting forward a low wage policy cloaked in the garb of a privately sponsored wages and incomes policy for the country at large'.[5] The eventual award made by the Brown Commission was close to that proposed by UNIP in its evidence, and was subsequently used by the government, as employer and fixer of minimum wages, to determine the level of wage increases to be implemented in other sectors.

The government's award of a pay increase to miners in 1975, nearly

18 months before the expiry of the existing pay agreement, is another example of its sensitivity to the strength of feelings in the union movement. For to ignore entirely such pressures would cause unionists to question the legitimacy of their union leadership, and might thereby eliminate an important channel through which UNIP attempts to maintain its supervision and regulation of trade union activity. Yet, the number of occasions on which the government and party are likely to intervene in this manner on the side of employees is steadily being reduced by the extension of public ownership over the former private sector. Consequently the government can do little to prevent itself becoming ever more strongly identified with the employers' side in wage negotiations.

If we accept the analysis that has just been presented—namely that the government's main concern in its relations with trade unions is to achieve political control of their activities, and that, to this end, the government is willing to concede a certain degree of liberality in settling pay claims—then the behaviour of the workers' representatives becomes easy to understand. For union leaders are torn between their duty to their electorate and the need to be seen to be loyal to government interests. At the uppermost levels of the trade union hierarchy it is the latter concern which is the more important, since the government has shown itself prepared to intervene forcefully to protect those officials that support it. It is not surprising, therefore, that in the key copper mining sector, union negotiators have not shown themselves willing to adopt militant negotiating postures, and have accepted pay offers (as in 1964, 1966, 1970 and 1974) which must have been significantly less generous than the employers and government would have been willing to have approved.

Finally, we have the union rank and file, who are confronted with a similar need to moderate large wage demands on account of political expediency. When the ruling party is confident of popular support (as in the period before 1969), rank and file militancy and unofficial action are tolerated. But when signs of political opposition are growing, such gestures of rank and file unrest are liable to be interpreted as acts of political hostility, and may be met by harsh counter measures.

At this point, we can usefully return to the question that gave rise to the discussion just presented, and try to draw some conclusions as to what actually does determine the rural/urban income differential. We shall do this by first eliminating a variety of factors which might be considered to influence the local wage scale but which appear not to have done so. The first such factor is the level of earnings in peasant agriculture, which in competitive models might be expected only to differ from average wages by an amount equal to 'the necessary extra costs of living in town rather than rural areas'. Not only have peasant incomes never been explicitly or implicitly mentioned during a wage award in Zambia, but the gap between peasant incomes and urban wages has been widening steadily since 1940.

The second factor which has not played any significant role in wage determination, although it was considered during both the Brown and O'Riordan Commission deliberations, is the relationship between wage increases and labour productivity gains. A third factor, 'the financial and economic circumstances' of Zambia, occurs regularly in the list of terms of reference of Salaries Commissions. Yet, there is no evidence whatever that a pessimistic forecast of the immediate economic prospects facing the country (such as that facing the O'Riordan or Mwanakatwe Salaries Commissions) has in any way reduced or altered the form of pay award. A fourth factor whose influence on wage determination we can dismiss as having been negligible is an official incomes policy. The policy formulated for Zambia lacks any statutory means of enforcement, and, even where the policy might be thought to have some moral force, as in the case of the O'Riordan Salaries Commission award, the government was prepared to resort to a dubious argument about the estimation of disposable income in order to circumvent the policy.

One final factor which, I would argue, has also not significantly affected the form of the eventual wage award is the Poverty Datum Line (PDL), the wage required to attain a minimum decent standard of living. The PDL is, in fact, the only measure outside the wage scale that has been considered as a basis for a pay award. It was considered, and rejected, by the 1964 Hadow Salaries Commission, but was later used by the Mwanakatwe Commission to justify its choice of K40 as the minimum monthly wage to be paid to public sector workers. However, it must be noted that an award of this size would, in any case, have been expected, bearing in mind the Commission's desire to take account of cost of living increases since 1971, and its intention of narrowing relative differentials. Thus, given the extremely crude method used to derive the PDL estimate of K40, one may be excused for suspecting that the 1975 award was made independently of the PDL figure. Only if future pay awards explicitly tie their minimum wage levels to the PDL (an unlikely event, considering the propensity of Salaries Commissions to give the lowest-paid workers pay increases somewhat in excess of those recorded in the cost of living) will it be correct to argue in support of the existence of a systematic relationship between the PDL and the wage scale.

Of all the many factors discussed in official reports of wage determination only three really seem to have influenced the eventual award. The first of these – wages in other sectors – can explain only relative wage differentials and not the absolute wage level. Accordingly, discussion of this factor is left until the next section of the chapter. The effect of the second factor – changes in the cost of living – is also somewhat difficult to evaluate in the context of the present discussion. Certainly, most awards for the past 15 years have been designed to ensure that an average worker receives an increase large enough to raise his real income above that at the time of the previous award. But this does nothing to help to explain how decisions are made regarding the size of the *increase* in real incomes, which will be equal to the amount by which wage increases exceed the rise in the cost of living.

We are left, therefore, with one factor – the state of industrial relations within the copper mining sector – to account for the major part of wage determination in Zambia. This may seem an arbitrary, ad hoc way in which to lump together all the other factors affecting wage levels and the rural/urban income differential. Yet if one is willing to accept the conclusions of the next section and supposes that the copper mining sector acts as a wage leader for all other sectors, one has to see the wage decision on the mines as the key event in Zambian wage determination.

Unfortunately, a concept like 'the state of industrial relations within the copper mining sector' is unwieldy from an analytical point of view. The description that has been given of the different objectives of the four main parties involved in mining pay negotiations demonstrates that it will not be easy to characterise all the issues that arise. In terms of methodology, the best approach to our characterisation of the 'state of industrial relations within the copper mining sector' will probably be as the solution of a problem in game theory. The employers want to minimise labour costs, subject to a restriction on the amount of labour unrest that their wage policy provokes; the MUZ Head Office is torn between loyalty to the rank and file members and the need to be seen to identify itself with government objectives; the MUZ individual members want higher wages, though not at the expense of a confrontation with the government. Finally, and most important of all at the present moment, there is the United National Independence Party whose immediate concern is to ensure political control over the trade union movement. Thus, the government's objectives as regards wage determination are largely decided by the nature of the political situation within Zambia. Where the threat of political opposition is perceived not to be serious (as before 1969), generous wage awards are felt to be an acceptable price to pay for trade union loyalty. Where, however, the internal political threat is acknowledged to be important, the government expects 'discipline' from trade unions. In this situation, the government is prepared only to grant sufficient wage increases (possibly no more than adequate to maintain real income levels) to prevent the established trade union leadership from becoming discredited. Wage awards made since 1969 must be seen in this light.

On the basis of an analysis of wage movements in Zambia over the past 15 years, we are drawn to the simple conclusion that the rate of change of the rural/urban income differential depends, above all, on one factor – the government perception of the threat of internal political unrest. When faced with signs of growing political opposition, the Zambian government has tended to react, not by wooing organised labour by offering large pay increases but by cracking down upon signs of unrest in the labour movement, and thus by reducing the real rate of wage increase enjoyed by wage earners. When, however, the threat of political opposition is judged to be remote, the government is prepared to tolerate dissent within the trade union movement, and is prepared, in consequence, to see workers obtain large real wage increases.

Sectoral Earnings Differentials

As regards 'pure' economics, our discussion of sectoral earnings differentials will be on rather firmer ground than the discussion of rural/urban income differentials which it follows. Sectoral differentials do appear to follow a fairly consistent pattern, with earnings highest in those sectors with the most to gain from reducing labour turnover, and with earnings also highest in the sectors with the lowest labour coefficients. Yet, in several respects, in particular as regards government intervention in the fixing of minimum wages, sectoral earnings differentials have a political origin.

Data on the levels and dates of change of certain key wage rates in different sectors are summarised in Tables 6.1 and 6.2, pages 128-31, and statistics on average sectoral earnings have been presented already in Chapter 3. From this material, several conclusions may be drawn. First, comparing earnings of unskilled workers, in different sectors, the relative earnings differentials have altered very little since 1960. We have taken the earnings of copper mining P5 underground workers to be the standard against which we compare all other wages, since P5 underground workers are the highest paid sizable group of semiskilled/

unskilled workers in Zambia. Expressing minimum wages in other sectors as a percentage of the earnings of P5 underground workers, we find that between 1961 and 1972 (before the next wage round got under way) railway wages remained unaltered at 33 per cent, workers on the general minimum wage remained on 35 per cent and daily paid government workers dropped slightly, from 33 to 31 per cent, while construction workers rose somewhat from 32 to 35 per cent. Local authority workers alone enjoyed a substantial gain, moving from 35 to 47 per cent, although this advantage had been almost entirely wiped out by 1975.

From Table 4.1, page 71, giving African earnings by sector, it is clear that average sectoral earnings have followed a more divergent path than their minimum wages. Transport, and to a lesser extent, manufacturing, finance, commerce and electricity sector wages grew faster than wages in other sectors. But these differences can quite convincingly be attributed to shifts in the structure of African employment within the sectors, rather than to differences in the rate of increase in the underlying pay scales. For example, in the transport sector, Africans moved rapidly into the jobs of lorry and railway drivers and became garage mechanics, causing a sharper shift in the distribution of employment towards more skilled jobs than has occurred in the agricultural, mining or construction sectors.

A final conclusion that we might draw from our data is that wage increases in most sectors occur in bursts at similar points of time. There is a clearly discernible wage round which takes place at intervals of three to four years, with one around 1963, another in 1966/7, another in 1970/1, and another in 1974/5. Within the wage round, the copper mines seem to be the leading sector. In 1963, the Morison award preceded the 1963/4 awards elsewhere. In 1966, the Brown Commission set the pattern for all subsequent pay rises. In 1970, the Zambia Railways and daily paid government workers' awards preceded that of the mines, but it could be argued that the Zambia Railways award was, in reality, the much delayed end of the 1966/7 wage round. In 1973, the mines award again came through before those for any other major sectors.

Knight[6] has tried to test the hypothesis that the mines act as a wage leading sector by means of regressions of N_t, annual absolute change in average earnings in non-mining sectors at time t, on M_t, annual absolute change in average earnings in the mining sector at time t, or on $M_{t-0.25}$ (at time t minus three months) or on $M_{t+0.25}$ (at time t plus three months). His two best equations, on the basis of 13 years' data, were

Table 6.1: Changes in Monthly Earnings in Various Jobs (K per month)

	Lowest-paid workers by industrial sector													
Year	Copper mining[c,a]	Railways[d]	Daily paid government labourers	Local authorities	Agriculture	Building industry[e]	General minimum wage[e]	P5 Under-[a] ground copper miners (formerly 'rockbreakers')	Mining plant operator[a,b] (concentrator)		Certified winding engine driver on mines[a]		Mining plant shift boss/ foreman[a]	
									Expatriate	Local	Expatriate	Local	Expatriate	Local
1961	28.68	17.50	15.38	16.47	(No minimum wage existed until 1964)	14.73	16.47	46.43	242.52	f	312.61	f	293.09	f
1962	33.38 (7/62)	17.50	15.38	16.47		14.73	16.47	50.81	243.88 (12/62)	f	313.16 (12/62)	f	293.59 (12/62)	f
1963	31.64	19.75 (3/63)	19.50 (7/63)	20.80 (7/63)		20.80 (7/63)	20.80 (7/63)	48.16	235.55	f	300.74	f	282.60	f
1964	39.13 (5/64)	25.60 (3/64)	19.50	23.00 (3/64)	11.05 (5/64)	20.80	20.80	67.80 (5/64)	258.51 (10/64)	f	329.70 (10/64)	f	276.67 (4/64)	f
1965	39.13	25.60	19.50	27.00	11.05	20.80	20.80	67.80	258.51	f	329.70	f	343.66 (7/65)	195.30 (4/65)
1966	57.33 (10/66)	25.60	19.50	27.00	11.05	20.80	20.80	87.43 (10/66)	258.51	137.34 (10/66)	329.70	165.48 (10/66)	343.66	238.25 (10/66)
1967	57.33	26.00	23.40 (1/67)	28.17 (1/67)	14.30 (11/67)	27.50 (4/67)	25.80 (4/67)	87.43	g	137.34	g	165.48	343.66	238.25
1968	57.33	26.00	23.40	30.00 (7/68)	14.30	27.50	25.80	87.43	g	137.34	g	165.48	343.66	238.25
1969	57.33	26.00	23.40	32.00 (5/69)	14.30	27.50	25.80	87.43	g	137.34	g	165.48	343.66	238.25
1970	57.33 (9/70)	30.00 (4/70)	28.50 (2/70)	32.00	14.30	27.50	25.80	95.55 (9/70)	g	116.55 (11/70)	g	144.37 (11/70)	404.78 (11/70)	238.88 (11/70)
1971	57.33	34.00	28.50	32.00	18.20 (10/71)	33.30 (9/71)	25.80	95.55	g	116.55	g	144.37	404.78	238.88
1972	57.33	36.00 (1/72)	28.50	43.00[h] (10/72)	18.20	33.30	33.30 (7/72)	95.55	g	116.55	g	144.37	404.78	238.88
1973	57.33	36.00	28.50	43.00[h]	18.20	33.30	33.30	106.05 (1/73)	g	131.25 (11/73)	g	160.12 (11/73)	488.25 (11/73)	271.95 (11/73)
1974	57.33	36.00	29.93 (7/74)	43.00	18.20	33.30	33.30	106.05	g	131.25	g	160.12	488.25	271.95
1975	67.73 (8/75)	36.00	40.00 (7/75)	43.00	18.20	33.30	33.30	116.55 (8/75)	g	147.00 (8/75)	g	181.12 (8/75)	561.75 (8/75)	308.70 (8/75)

[a]The various bonuses paid to copper miners have been consolidated into earnings in deriving these figures.
[b]This was the lowest paid category of European workers on the mines!
[c]This group were called 'Group I Surface Workers' until 1964, then they became 'Surface Workmen', and in 1970 'Grade PI Surface Workers .
[d]This group consists of 'Group A Statutory Industrial Council Railway Workers'.
[e]Statutory minimum wages for workers in other sectors moved more in tune with that for building workers than with the general minimum wage.
[f]A local scale for these jobs is not available for earlier years. In some cases, there was no comparable job in the local scale.
[g]These jobs were Zambianised soon after 1966. Hence the expatriate scale was not altered after 1966, and soon became redundant.
[h]This award applied only to local councils in urban areas. The Minister of Local Government and Housing refused to extend the award to employees of rural councils.

Table 6.1—Continued

Year	Primary school teachers (Form II + 2 years training)	Civil Service Clerical Officer (Div. I) with 'O'-level certificate	Railway clerk general grade[i,k] (min/max)	Railway assistant foreman = chargeman[i,k] (min/max)	Railway Group F SIC worker[k,l] (min/max)	Building worker minimum wage[m] (wage for skilled worker)	Starting wage grade 9[k,n] (daily paid government worker)	Starting wage grade 4[p] (daily paid government worker)
1961	41.67	73.33	56.20/177.30	179.00	27.50/48.25	17.93	21.02	35.75
1962	41.67	73.33	63.50/200.33	179.00	27.50/48.25	17.93	21.02	35.75
1963	41.67	73.33	63.50/200.33	202.12	29.75/50.50	30.48 (7/63)	21.02	35.75
1964	55.83 (1/64)	68.00 (1/64)	63.50/200.33	191.00/220.83	35.80/57.30	30.48	22.75	93.60
1965	55.83	68.00	76.17/240.33	229.17/265.00	35.80/57.30	30.48	29.25	93.60
1966	55.83	68.00	76.17/240.33	229.17/265.00	35.80/57.30	30.48	29.25	93.60
1967	82.00 (1/67)	86.10 (1/67)	76.17/240.33	229.17/265.00	42.50/58.00	50.92 (4/67)	34.32	93.10
1968	82.00	86.10	76.17/240.33	229.17/265.00	42.50/58.00	50.92	34.32	93.10
1969	82.00	86.10	76.17/240.33	229.17/265.00	46.50/62.00	50.92	34.32	93.10
1970	82.00	86.10	76.17/240.33	229.17/265.00	46.50/62.00	50.92	39.60	99.90
1971	93.00 (5/71)	101.00 (5/71)	83.16/247.33	225.16/305.38	50.50/66.00	53.16 (9/71)	39.60	99.90
1972	93.00	101.00	83.16/247.33	225.17/305.38	53.00/69.50	58.16	39.60	99.90
1973	93.00	101.00	83.16/247.33	225.17/305.38	53.00/69.50	58.16	39.60	99.90
1974	93.00	101.00	83.16/247.33	225.17/305.38	53.00/69.50	58.16	41.52 (7/74)	104.90 (7/74)
1975	128.00 (7/75)	128.00 (7/75)	83.16/247.33	225.17/305.38	53.00/69.50	58.16	53.00 (7/75)	128.00 (7/75)

[i] These two jobs are in the National Industrial Council (former European) scale.

[k] The exact months of wage increases are not known. The figures quoted are year-end wage rates.

[l] This constitutes the highest paid group of workers in the Statutory Industrial Council (former African) scale.

[m] This represents the statutory minimum wage for a skilled building worker, as agreed in the Building Industry's Joint Industrial Council. The tool allowance (6s per month until 1962, 10s per month until 1971, and K2 per month in 1972) has been counted as part of the monthly earnings.

[n] Grade 9 represents the lowest paid group of trade tested daily paid government workers.

[p] Grade 4 represents the highest paid group of trade tested daily paid government workers.

Sources: Derived from 1960-1973 *Annual Reports* of the Department of Labour; from Appendices and the Main text of the Report of the Brown Commission, 1966; from the Report of the Hadow Commission, 1966; from the Report of the O'Riordan Salaries Commission; from information from Copper Industry Service Bureau; from the Report of the Mwanakatwe Salaries Commission; and from discussions with officials of the Ministry of Labour and Social Services, Lusaka.

Table 6.2: Monthly Wages Expressed as Percentage of Wage of 'P5 Underground' Copper Miners

Year	Lowest-paid workers by industrial sector: Copper mining	Railway	Daily paid government	Local authorities	Agriculture	Building industry	General minimum wage	Primary school teacher (Form II + 2 years training)	Mining plant operator (concentrator): Expatriate	Mining plant operator (concentrator): Local	Certificated winding engine driver on mines: Expatriate	Certificated winding engine driver on mines: Local
1961	62	38	33	35	–	32	35	90	522	a	673	a
1962	66	34	30	32	–	29	32	82	480	a	616	a
1963	66	41	40	43	–	43	43	87	489	a	624	a
1964	58	38	29	34	16	31	31	82	381	a	486	a
1965	58	38	29	40	16	31	31	82	381	a	486	a
1966	66	29	22	31	13	24	24	64	296	157	377	189
1967	66	30	27	32	16	31	30	94	b	157	b	189
1968	66	30	27	34	16	31	30	94	b	157	b	189
1969	66	30	27	37	16	31	30	94	b	157	b	189
1970	60	33	31	35	15	30	28	86	b	122	b	151
1971	60	37	31	35	17	35	28	97	b	122	b	151
1972	60	38	31	47	19	35	35	97	b	122	b	151
1973	54	34	27	41	17	31	31	87	b	124	b	151
1974	54	34	28	41	17	31	31	88	b	124	b	151
1975	58	31	34	37	16	29	29	110	b	126	b	155

Table 6.2: cont.

Year	Mining Plant shift boss/foreman		Civil Service Clerical Officer Div. I with 'O'-level certificate	Railway clerk (General Grade) (min/max)	Railway chargemen artisan-foremen (min/max)	Railway SIC worker, Group F (min/max)	Minimum wage skilled building workers	Grade 9 daily paid government workers	Grade 4 daily paid government workers
	Expatriate	Local							
1961	631	a	158	122/383	386	59/104	39	45	77
1962	578	a	144	125/395	386	54/95	35	41	70
1963	587	a	152	131/416	419	62/105	63	44	74
1964	408	a	100	94/296	282/326	53/85	45	34	138
1965	507	288	100	111/355	339/391	53/85	45	43	138
1966	393	273	78	87/276	261/303	41/66	35	33	107
1967	393	273	98	87/276	261/303	49/66	58	39	106
1968	393	273	98	87/276	261/303	49/66	58	39	106
1969	393	273	98	87/276	261/303	53/71	58	39	106
1970	424	250	90	80/253	240/277	49/65	53	41	104
1971	424	250	106	87/259	268/320	53/69	61	41	104
1972	424	250	106	87/259	268/320	56/73	61	41	104
1973	460	256	95	78/233	212/288	50/66	55	37	94
1074	460	256	95	78/233	212/288	50/66	55	39	99
1975	482	265	110	71/212	193/262	45/60	50	45	110

[a] A local scale for these jobs is not available for earlier years. In some cases, there was no comparable job in the local scale.

[b] These jobs were Zambianised soon after 1966. Hence the expatriate scale was not altered after 1966, and soon became redundant.

Sources: Derived from 1960-1973 *Annual Reports* of the Department of Labour; from Appendices and the Main text of the Report of the Brown Commission, 1966; from the Report of the Hadow Commission, 1966; from the Report of the O'Riordan Salaries Commission; from information from Copper Industry Service Bureau; from the Report of the Mwanakatwe Salaries Commission; and from discussions with officials of the Ministry of Labour and Social Services, Lusaka. (For full titles of O'Riordan and Mwanakatwe Commissions, see Ch. 5, Refs 11 and 12.)

$$N_t = 2.844 + 0.289M_t \qquad (R^2 = 0.632)$$
$$\text{(SE 0.070)}$$

and

$$N_t = 2.023 + 0.329M_{t-0.25} \qquad (R^2 = 0.601)$$
$$(0.089)$$

The equation regressing N_t on $M_{t+0.25}$ had a slightly lower R^2 value. Yet, this is far from conclusive evidence that the mines are wage leaders. Not only was R^2 highest in the equation with no lags, but the method of calculating $M_{t-0.25}$ (taking it to be $0.75M_t + 0.25M_{t-1}$) is of doubtful validity and begs the key question of when, within the year, the pay increases occurred.

Therefore one must rely upon impressionistic evidence on wage leadership and on the wage round to support the view of the mines as the wage leading sector. This role tends to reinforce the mineworkers' ability as a homogeneous labour force, represented by a powerful union, to maintain their earnings above those of similar workers in other sectors. But the main factors behind the premium enjoyed by miners over other workers must be the 'pure' economic ones mentioned at the beginning of this section. Ever since the late 1920s, the mining companies have invested heavily in social services and training expenditures designed to reduce labour turnover. As Table 5.2, page 106, indicates, the labour turnover has been brought down to remarkably low levels. To maintain this level, the mines have to be kept more attractive than rival employers. In terms of training costs per worker, the transport sector probably follows the mines, and hence has the next greatest interest in stabilising its labour force. At the bottom of the list in training costs per worker, one expects to find the agricultural sector, with possibly the construction sector above it. It is not surprising then, to find that the mines pay their workers the highest wages, followed by the transport sector. Agricultural workers receive the lowest pay, with the construction workers the next above them.

The mines have an added reason for paying high wages to their employees, since labour costs per unit of output and labour co-efficients are lower than in any other major employment sector. The mines are thus better placed than other sectors to absorb higher wages. In 1967, for example, the direct wage and salary bill accounted for 18.6 per cent of the value of gross output in the copper mining sector (10.3 per cent being paid to African workers and 8.3 per cent to expatriates). In the non-mining sector the comparable figure was 30.9 per cent (19.8 per cent going to Africans and 11.1 per cent to expatriates).

Since there is clear evidence that wages in all sectors move in step with one another, and that the mines set the lead for other sectors, it is the total (direct and indirect) labour costs rather than merely the direct labour costs which are more important as a determinant of a sector's ability to concede pay increases. In 1965, Knight derived the information given in Table 6.3, below, of the wage component in total costs in the different sectors. Using more recent (1967) data, I have derived estimates

Table 6.3: The Wage Component of Costs, 1965

Sector	Direct and indirect wage costs as percentage of gross output
Peasant farming, fishing, forestry and quarrying	1
Commercial farming	40
Metal mining	27
Manufacturing sector	18-34
Construction	34
Electricity and water	42
Trade	33
Banks, real estate	35
Transport	44
Other services	84
Total economy	34

Source: J.B. Knight, 'Wages and Zambia's Economic Development' in C. Elliott (ed.), *Constraints*, Table 4.4, p. 106.

of the direct and indirect labour coefficients per K1,000 of final demand for different sectors' products (see Table 3.14, pages 67-8), and it is useful to note that, like Knight's figures, the copper mines display a low labour coefficient, the manufacturing sectors follow next, and are in turn followed by the commerce, transport, construction, services and farming sectors, in that order. It is no surprise that this happens to correspond closely to a ranking of these sectors in terms of decreasing wages.

But while the ranking of sectoral earnings is consistent with the underlying use of labour and distribution of skill between sectors, there is reason to believe that, among the lowest-paid workers at any rate, the sectoral differentials are narrower than the unfettered play of free market forces would imply. This is on account of government intervention in minimum wage determination, which has tended to create just three minimum wages, in the modern sector: the minimum wage in copper mining, which is entirely determined by collective bargaining in that sector; the minimum wage for all other non-agricultural workers, of which some are the result of collective bargaining and others are fixed by government action, but which are all similar to one another; and the government-fixed agricultural minimum wage. In the view of the Ministry of Labour and Social Services, minimum wage orders should be used to narrow the differential between earnings in the various non-mining urban sectors and to narrow the gap between agricultural and non-agricultural wages. To this end the ministry has intervened to reduce minimum wage awards agreed upon by Joint Industrial Councils (JICs) in sectors such as engineering and the motor trade, which were prepared to fix minimum wages above those in other sectors.[7] On the other hand, the ministry was prepared to go to the Cabinet for approval of the generous 1971 agricultural minimum wage award which violated the 5 per cent norm of the current incomes policy.

In these respects, political/social welfare considerations outweighed the economic considerations mentioned above. Yet, minimum wage determination apart, the conclusions of the earlier part of this section remain generally true, and sectoral wage differentials are best explained in terms of underlying differences between the training costs and labour intensity of production in different sectors.

The Skilled/Unskilled Differential

There are important practical difficulties to be overcome before we can discuss the movement of the skilled/unskilled differential. These arise out of the fact that, at higher income levels, fringe benefits typically come to account for a large share of real earnings. Consequently, our discussion will be divided into two parts—an analysis of the trend in the money salary/wage differential, and a study of the trend in fringe benefits.

As regards the monetary wage/salary differential, Tables 6.1 and 6.2 suggest that the gap between the earnings of unskilled workers and the earnings of the lower-paid white-collar staff (as represented by junior railway clerks or primary school teachers) has remained unchanged or narrowed over the past 15 years. Between unskilled workers and more senior white-collar staff (such as Civil Service Clerical Officers, Division 1, or Railway Clerks), however, the evidence of Tables 6.1 and 6.2 is that monetary differentials have narrowed appreciably.

In the two most important sectors, the copper mines and public administration, the pattern of the narrowing of the unskilled/white-collar differentials has been somewhat different. On the mines, staff grade workers suffered relative to other workers during the 1964 NRAMU/United Mineworkers' Union struggle, when they were powerless to prevent their salaries from being 'localised' into new, lower local scales separated from expatriate scales. In addition, the staff grades gained somewhat less from the 1970 and 1975 awards than other mineworkers. But the 1962, 1966 and 1973 mining pay awards granted more or less equal percentage increases throughout the scale.

In contrast, Civil Service Salaries Commissions have taken the narrowing of wage/salary differentials to be a deliberate objective. The 1963/4 Hadow Salaries Commission, while granting generous pay increases to wage earners, actually reduced salaries at the top of the scale, in line with the recommendations of the UN/ECA/FAO (United Nations/Economic Commission for Africa/Food and Agriculture Organisation) Seers Mission of that period. The reduction of inequality remained an objective of the 1966 Whelan Salaries Commission and appeared among that commission's terms of reference. Accordingly, while the Brown Commission of the same date granted equal percentage increases to all mineworkers, the Hadow Commission tapered its awards in a manner very much to the advantage of lower-paid workers. The 1971 O'Riordan and 1975 Mwanakatwe Salaries Commissions continued, less zealously, their predecessors' mission of reducing income inequalities.

In many sectors, a narrowing of the salary/wage gap may reflect pressures towards egalitarianism from the (unskilled) bulk of trade union members or from government policy makers. But in a macroeconomic context, the narrowing reflects more the lessening imbalance between the supply of and demand for skilled labour in the economy. The fact that differentials have been reduced more rapidly in the Civil Service than on the copper mines would tend to support the macroeconomic interpretation, since the supply of skilled clerical and administrative Zambian staff, of the type in demand in the Civil Service, has expanded much more rapidly since 1960 than the supply of skilled technicians, artisans and engineers required on the mines.

A careful examination of Tables 6.1 and 6.2 provides further reason for considering the wage/salary and skilled/unskilled differentials to have a basis in the changing pattern of local labour supplies. If we look at the trend in the wages of public sector employees between 1961 and 1972, as given by columns 3, 4, 8, 11, 16 and 17 of Table 6.2, we observe that the differentials between the earnings of unskilled workers (columns 3 and 4), and the lowest semi-skilled workers (column 16), and white collar workers with low secondary school qualifications (column 8) have altered little – a result which corresponds well with the fact that all of these jobs have been filled locally without undue difficulty throughout the period in question. Yet, when we study the trend in the earnings of more senior white-collar staff (column 11) and more skilled black-collar workers (column 17), we note a remarkable shift in relative incomes, particularly around the time of independence. While the supply of Form Five secondary school leavers, with the necessary qualifications for senior clerical posts, has more than kept pace with the growth in demand, the supply of fully qualified local artisans has failed to meet all local needs. Consequently the ratio of senior clerical salaries to artisan wages in the public sector (columns 11 and 17) had dropped from 2:1 to 1:1 in a decade.

In the building sector, which like the public sector displayed a very rapid growth rate in employment in the period covered in the tables, we again observe (columns 6 and 15) how workers at the lower end of the skilled black-collar employment categories have been able to improve their position vis-à-vis unskilled workers during the decade under review.

The railways wage data (columns 2, 12, 13 and 14) help to complete the picture of changing differentials in the context of changing labour supplies and demands. Comparing unskilled and semi-skilled workers (columns 2 and 14), differentials have narrowed slightly (though more markedly at the wage maximum within the skill categories). This narrowing is probably a result, in part, of a much slower growth in the demand for skilled artisans than was experienced in the construction or public sectors. Higher up the scale (columns 12 and 13), it is evident that the differentials enjoyed by skilled over unskilled workers have been reduced appreciably. But, even so, the wage differentials received by skilled white-collar staff have fallen faster than those for comparable black-collar workers.

The frequent changes in grading schemes on the mines make it difficult to produce comparable statistics of skilled miners' earnings for comparison in Table 6.2. However, the changes in mining pay scales since 1961 appear to follow the pattern of railway earnings, rather than public sector or construction earnings.

This discussion helps to point to some tentative conclusions about the evolution of white-collar/black-collar and skilled/unskilled monetary earnings differentials since 1961. The gaps between the earnings of unskilled workers and the lower skilled black-collar grades have risen, or remained constant according to a division of sectors of employment into rapidly growing (i.e. construction and public service) or slow growing (such as Zambia Railways and the copper mines). In addition, in every sector, at the lower levels, black-collar monetary earnings grew faster than white-collar earnings.

Higher up the scale of skills, we still find that black-collar earnings grew more rapidly than those for white-collar staff; but relative to unskilled workers' wages, both have fallen since 1961. This can be explained by the steady Zambianisation of senior white-collar and black-collar posts which has occurred faster in the former than the latter. As Zambianisation proceeded, local pay scales fell further behind those that had to be offered to expatriate employees, and thus affected white-collar employees more severely than artisans.

We must not forget, however, that money earnings are only a proportion of total incomes, and that at the highest income levels, the value of fringe benefits, such as housing allowances, pension rights, Provident Fund contributions and travel allowances, may rival the value of monetary wages. Evidence on fringe benefits is notoriously difficult to collect. In the parastatal sector, for example, there appears to be a number of pay scales in operation for senior staff, with fringe benefits to some extent determined by the recipients themselves; and popular mythology would attribute a very high, and rapidly growing, value to these benefits. Unfortunately, the only set of fringe benefits on which there exists a reasonable literature is that of Civil Service housing allowances. Accordingly we will analyse their determination, and attempt to derive some broad conclusions from the analysis.

Before 1964, the Civil Service housing arrangements involved the provision of housing to all civil servants at a subeconomic rental of 12.5 per cent of their basic salary, but with an upper limit on rental payments of £225 per annum. The quality of housing varied with salary levels, with the result that, up to incomes of £1,800 per annum, the value of housing subsidies might have been considered to have risen proportionally with income. At income levels above £1,800 per annum, rents remained fixed at £225, so that the value of housing subsidies grew more rapidly than incomes.

The 1963-4 Hadow Commission was asked in its terms of reference to consider 'modifications to the existing system whereby public officers and teachers are provided with housing at sub-economic rentals, with a view to encouraging civil servants to provide their own accommodation as far as possible'[8]; but the commission saw little purpose in moving to a system of economic rentals while the supply of housing was 'far from adequate'. It did recommend ending the £225 upper limit on rental payments, but the recommendation was not accepted, although no reasons were given for the decision. House rentals did not appear in the 1966 Whelan Commission's terms of reference. Nevertheless the commission felt obliged to discuss the problem of subsidised housing, and came to the same general conclusions as its predecessor. The 1969 Rogers Report, *Education in Transition*, on conditions in the teaching service, also took the view that a system of economic rentals was possible only with a considerably expanded supply of housing.

The 1971 O'Riordan Salaries Commission was presented with the identical terms of reference on housing to the Hadow Commission. And like the Hadow Commission, it recommended removing the platform on rental payments, and wanted to move gradually towards a scheme of economic rentals. The government seemed to prefer stronger action and proposed to transfer most government housing to the Zambia National Building Society or the National Housing Authority. It said it would instruct these organisations to grant 100 per cent mortgages for the purchase of houses at market prices, or to rent out the houses at economic rentals. Civil servants were to receive salary increases of up to 20 per cent to compensate them for the extra rental payments.

The government's proposals were cited as a major reason for granting Permanent Secretaries wage increases in excess of the incomes policy 5 per cent norm, but, faced with the administrative problems of implementing the changeover, the far-reaching reforms advocated in the Government Paper were quietly dropped in favour of the lifting of the platform on housing rentals and the establishment of a new rental scale fixed at 15 per cent of gross salary. In 1974, the rental increase was rescinded, and house rentals reverted to the level of 12.5 per cent of gross salary ruling before 1971. In 1975, the Mwanakatwe Commission went even further against the spirit of the O'Riordan recommendations and raised the value of housing allowances. It reduced rentals to 10 per cent of income for high-cost housing, 8 per cent for medium-cost, and 6 per cent for low-cost housing.

Between 1960 and 1975 therefore, we observe that the system of housing subsidies has altered slightly in an egalitarian direction, with the abolition of the K450 limit on annual rentals, and the drop in rentals as a proportion of income devised so as to favour most the low-paid workers living in low-cost housing. If other fringe benefits moved in line with housing subsidies, we can conclude that the trend in monetary wage/salary differentials fairly reflected the trend in overall wage/salary differentials. Since the evidence presented above shows that monetary wage/salary differentials have narrowed over the past 15 years, we have reason to believe that, whether as a result of egalitarian pressures from unskilled workers or government policy makers or as a consequence of the working of the law of supply and demand for skilled labour, the real differentials between skilled and unskilled workers' wages in the modern sector have grown smaller in relative terms since 1950.

Conclusions

Throughout this chapter we have attempted to analyse the racial, sectoral and skill differentials in the wage scale and have tried to identify those features of present and past wage scales which can be explained in terms of 'purely economic' phenomena and those features for which the only valid explanation is a political one. From our analysis it would appear that the purely economic phenomena are most important in determining sectoral and skill differentials. We have presented evidence to demonstrate that the copper mines act as a wage leader for all other sectors, and that the differences in wage rates in different sectors reflect very closely the differences that exist in the labour intensity of production (with the highest wages being paid by the sectors with the lowest labour intensities, and vice versa). Sectoral differentials also appear to correspond closely to the training costs incurred by employers and the benefits that accrue to them from stabilisation.

As regards skill differentials, they have narrowed in most sectors, except possibly for salaries at the very top of the scale. Fringe benefits, although considerable, do not seem to have moved so as to affect the decrease in monetary skill differentials. Such evidence as is available shows that skill differentials have narrowed more rapidly in the case of clerical and administrative jobs, for which there is an ample supply of local candidates, than in the case of technical and scientific jobs, where local qualified staff is still scarce.

However, when we come to consider the determinants of the average level of urban wages in relation to rural earnings, or of the racial wage differential, we have to conclude that political factors are the most important. This is not to deny that they are important also in determining other differentials. For example, we have seen that government intervention in minimum wage determination has tended recently to narrow sectoral differentials. But virtually the entire period since 1940 has been one in which political factors (such as the relations between the mining companies, the white miners, African miners and the government of the day, or the battle between the government, the unions and opposition parties for the allegiance of the mineworkers) have dominated the determination of expatriate/local differentials and rural/urban differentials. Rather than those differentials being determined as a result of the working of a competitive economic model in the labour market, employers have reacted, instead, to the wage rates fixed by the interaction of political forces, by adjusting their factor proportions so as to maximise profits.[9]

The future course of wage determination is hard to predict. On the one hand, the defusing of the vexed issue of expatriate/local differentials and the creation of a one party state might both be thought to reduce the impact of political factors on wage fixing. But on the other hand, growing government participation in the economy will involve the administration more directly in wage negotiations, and might be felt to increase the possibilities of political intervention in wage determination. My own feeling is that, while the latter is likely to be true in the short term, say up to 1980, in the longer term the government will see its interests in a centralised economy to lie more in the direction of lowering labour costs. In that event, we may expect to see the determination of wages in Zambia conforming increasingly to a competitive model.

Notes

1. M. Burawoy, *The Colour of Class on the Copper Mines*, Zambian Paper No. 7 (Institute for African Studies, Lusaka, 1972).
2. G. Arrighi, 'Labour Supplies in Historical Perspective: A study of the Proletarianization of the African Peasantry in Rhodesia', *Journal of Development Studies*, vol. 6, no. 3 (April 1970), p. 222.
3. See, for example, E.A.G. Robinson, 'The Organisation of African Mine Workers', Ch. X, in J. Merle Davis (ed.), *Modern Industry and the African* (Frank Cass, London, 1967).
4. A. L. Epstein, *Politics in an Urban African Community* (Manchester University Press, Manchester, 1958); K. Quinn, 'Industrial Relations in Zambia: 1935-1969', in C. Elliott (ed.), *Constraints on the Economic Development of Zambia* (Oxford University Press, Nairobi, 1971); R.H. Bates, *Unions, Parties and Political Development: A Study of Mineworkers in Zambia* (Yale University Press, New Haven, 1971).
5. *Report of the Commission of Inquiry into the Mining Industry* (Brown Commission Report) (Government Printer, Lusaka, 1966), para. 102.
6. J.B. Knight, 'Wages and Zambia's Economic Development', in C. Elliott (ed.), *Constraints on the Economic Development of Zambia* (Oxford University Press, Nairobi, 1971).
7. In some cases the ministry reduced JIC awards in 1971 from a 35 per cent increase to one of only 12 per cent.
8. *Report of the Commission Appointed to Review the Salaries and Conditions of Service of the Northern Rhodesia Public and Teaching Services, and of the Northern Rhodesia Army and Air Force* (Hadow Commission Report) (Government Printer, Lusaka, 1964), p. i, para. iv.
9. See R.E. Baldwin, *Economic Development and Export Growth* (University of California Press, Los Angeles, 1966), and J.M. Mwanza, 'Modern Sector Employment Growth' (unpublished PhD Thesis, Cornell University, 1973).

7 PRICES AND INCOMES POLICY – A COMPARATIVE ANALYSIS

In earlier chapters, we have had to consider many aspects of official policy on wages, incomes and prices. The fact that the discussion has been spread over so many chapters is, in part, a reflection of the disparate, unco-ordinated nature of incomes policy in Zambia. Yet there has emerged in Zambia, as in other Eastern African countries, a growing sense in which the government seeks to project its policies on all aspects of income distribution as being governed by a single prices and incomes policy. Administrative machinery (an Industrial Court, a Prices Board and a Productivity, Wages and Prices Council) has been proposed or established to implement the policy. In this chapter, we shall compare the experiences of Zambia, Tanzania and Kenya in this field; and in the final chapter, we shall examine the main components required if an incomes policy is to attain its goals.

By 'incomes policy' we understand a unified policy on the distribution of income. Thus an incomes policy will be greatly concerned with matters like price control, the size and taxation of profits, the determination of rural incomes, the relationship between rural and urban incomes, and the structure of wage incomes and salaries above the minimum wage level. To some extent, an incomes policy may be considered to be interested in who actually receives the incomes; for example, the policy may distinguish between the treatment of incomes according to whether they are earned by local or foreign individuals and institutions or whether an institution is co-operatively or privately owned. In its dynamic aspects, an incomes policy will, in addition, have to be concerned with employment creation.

For the purposes of the present discussion, we shall restrict the scope of our analysis to policy on prices, labour incomes and profits, excluding consideration of those respects in which the policy distinguishes on nationalistic or ideological grounds between the treatment of local and foreign individuals and companies. Employment creation policy will also receive scant attention in our discussion, not because it deserves to be overlooked, but because it would be impossible to do justice to it in the space available.

In terms of this chapter, therefore, we can treat incomes policy as consisting of five main components: (i) agricultural pricing and production policy, (ii) price control, (iii) profits taxation, (iv) minimum wage determination, and (v) the control of wages and salaries above the minimum.

Where, as in Eastern Africa, the majority of the population depends on agriculture for its livelihood, and the majority of national income comes from company profits, one might suppose that the most important element of incomes policy would be agricultural pricing and production policy, followed by profit taxation. Minimum wage determination, with its influence on the size of the rural/urban income differential, would be ranked the third most important component, followed by control of wages above the minimum; and price control, a policy of most doubtful effectiveness, would be in last place.

In fact, a ranking of these components in terms of the importance attached to them in official incomes policy appears to run in an almost exactly reverse order to that hypothesised above. Governments dominated by, and responding to, urban, largely middle-class, interests experience strong pressures for price controls. Since rising labour costs force up prices, the governments can secure a measure of popular support for wage controls in the context of price controls. Profit taxation, having little influence on consumer price levels, is determined in the light of broad judgements about what local and foreign investors are willing to tolerate; while agricultural producer prices are manipulated more so as to hold down the urban cost of living than to improve the rural/urban distribution of income.

The gap between the theory and the practice of incomes policy is clearly considerable. In the remainder of this chapter we shall consider first the theoretical aspects of incomes policy, and then the practice of the policies in Zambia, Tanzania and Kenya. In Chapter 8, we shall discuss how the two can be reconciled.

The Theory of Incomes Policy

Agricultural Pricing and Production Policy

In the absence of an effective system of negative income taxes for low-paid workers and self-employed farmers, agricultural pricing policy is one of the best ways available to government policy makers through which they can influence the real incomes of farmers. The difficulty in using agricultural pricing policy arises out of the need to tailor it so that the target groups of the lowest-paid farmers gain, rather than high-income commercial farmers. In addition, one has to take careful account of the manner in which, say, raising the producer prices of goods produced by small-scale farmers distorts the entire economy.

In the short run, higher producer prices for the products of small farmers will, if their effect is not entirely eroded by inflation, require a real decrease in urban wages or in government expenditure, or a reduction in foreign reserves. They will also tend to distort the patterns of production in both the small and large farming sectors as between products receiving a subsidy and products receiving no subsidy or a lower one. Thus one will find, for example, that an increase in the producer price of maize, designed to boost the earnings of small farmers, will, if not entirely financed by higher subsidies, reduce the real earnings of urban maize consumers, and at the same time distort the production of small and large farmers (whom it would be difficult to prevent from sharing in the higher prices) away from other crops towards maize.

The redistributive and distortionary effects of an agricultural subsidy will also affect the volume and the composition of investment. A higher maize price will reduce real savings in the urban sector while increasing the savings of the rural population. If the marginal propensities to save of urban workers exceed those of the beneficiaries from the higher maize price, the overall volume of investment (and thus, one presumes, the future growth of the economy) will fall. On the debit side, the economy will have to accept a slower rate of growth, while, on the credit side, a growing share of the profits from investment will accrue to farmers. If, however, farmers tend to save more than the people who will finance the higher maize price,[1] the economy will enjoy both more rapid growth and a larger share of the benefits from this growth passing to the rural population.

From a macroeconomic point of view, these are probably the most important dynamic implications of raising agricultural producer prices, but there is also a dynamic distortionary effect from increasing investment in, say, maize production at the expense of other investment, and this must be taken into account.

The full analysis of all these implications will be a complicated task, and the conclusions will depend crucially upon the exact nature of the welfare judgements that policy makers choose to make. Elsewhere,[2] I have investigated the results of using a long-run planning model for the Zambian economy to derive optimal subsidy schedules, taking account of both the short-run and long-run repercussions of the subsidies. As one would expect, the nature of the subsidy schedules depends very much on one's assumptions about the form of the government's social welfare function and such features as the strength of its aversion to income inequality.

The other main aspect of agricultural policy in the context of incomes policy concerns the structure of production. The distribution of production between large and small producers is, in part, a reflection of the pattern of producer prices; but one important portion of agricultural production, that consumed by a farmer's own family, is very little affected by producer pricing policy. Consequently, if a government wishes to raise the income of a household producing largely for its own consumption, other policies, directed primarily at the encouragement of production independently of price incentives, will be required. The precise form that these will take depends upon the structure of extension services within the country. However, it is certain that it will involve a marked shift in emphasis, away from the provision of extension services for successful, 'progressive' farmers, towards extension services focused upon the poorest, least successful agricultural households. In theoretical terms, the necessary shift in objective may be characterised as one away from a growth-oriented concern with maximisation of GNP towards one closer to a Rawlsian[3] maximin approach to distributive justice, in which overrising importance is placed upon maximising the incomes of the poorest household in the population.

Price Control

Despite the prominence given to consumer price control in the formulation of so many official incomes policies, there is little theoretical support for this emphasis. Given ideal conditions, price control could play a role in reducing excess profits in some sectors, but, even then, from a theoretical point of view, it would be simpler to use, instead, a system of taxes and subsidies to correct the pattern of income distribution. However, conditions for price control are generally far from ideal. The administrative apparatus to enforce price control does not exist; black markets develop; and, where price control is fairly effective, it is impossible to force manufacturers to produce, or farmers to grow, or retailers to stock loss-making items. In other words, price control is not only a cumbersome instrument to use to correct the distribution of income, but it is also liable to veer either towards under-enforcement, in which case it is ineffective, or towards overzealous enforcement, in which case products cease to be available.

Profit Taxation

There are several schools of thought about private investment in developing countries. There are people who believe that all private enterprise and private property represent exploitation. Either private property must be eliminated, or 100 per cent profit taxation must be introduced. Another school of thought, reflecting to varying degrees the official policies of most Eastern African governments, believes that private investment has to be tolerated in a number of sectors for the capital, skills and technology that it provides. Some sectors may be reserved for government ownership, while others are declared open only to joint government-private partnerships, while yet others are effectively reserved for private investment.

Where private investment is tolerated, there arises the question of how best to tax the profits earned in the private sector. This, in turn, depends on four main factors: the size of the economic rent earned in a sector; the manner in which profits are distributed; the proportion re-invested; and the premium that a government is willing to pay to attract modern skills and technology.

With these considerations in mind, the most appropriate treatment of profits would seem to be to devise an excess profits tax to come into operation once the rate of return on capital exceeded the transfer earnings of capital plus an acceptable premium paid to attract skills and technology. If an excess profits tax is opposed on administrative grounds, exchange control regulations and withholding taxes can be employed to encourage foreign investors to keep their 'excess profits' within the country for reinvestment. However, should an excess profits tax be rejected, the position of profits earned by domestic capital would remain unsatisfactory. For a real danger would exist that low levels of taxation of profits would exacerbate existing income and wealth inequality, without yielding any offsetting advantages in the form of, say, a higher rate of domestic capital accumulation.

The taxation of mining profits in Zambia must be close to the ideal just described. Private shareholders face a marginal (and average) tax rate of 78.5 per cent on distributed profits before exchange-control restrictions may reduce foreign shareholders' receipts further; but these tax rates do not come into effect until the net, post-tax return on capital is at least 12 per cent per annum. Private investors are thereby assured an acceptable return on their capital, and are offered some incentives for efficient production, while the government shares handsomely in the excess profits earned during periods of high commodity prices.

Minimum Wage Determination

Minimum wage determination plays a dual key role in the unfolding of the pattern of income distribution. On the one hand, the minimum wage, more than any other single factor, determines the size of the rural/urban gap facing unskilled workers, and thereby affects the inflow of rural migrants into towns. On the other hand, the minimum wage exerts a considerable influence on the structure of wages above the legal minimum. Berg has estimated that one half of all wages in Africa are determined directly by the minimum wage.[4] The International Labour Office (ILO) has distinguished between three underlying criteria in minimum wage determination: (i) 'wages paid for comparable work elsewhere in the economy or, more generally, the standard of living of other social groups'; (ii) 'the needs of workers'; and (iii) 'the capacity to pay'.[5] Of these, the first finds much the greatest academic support.

(i) 'Comparable Incomes'. According to criterion (i),[6] both considerations of social equity and the need to limit rural-urban migration make it hard to justify paying urban wage workers more than they could have earned (with some allowances for the extra costs of urban, as opposed to rural, life) in the rural areas. In more technical terms, such authors are arguing that the shadow price, or the opportunity cost, of creating a job for an urban wage earner is closely related to the average or marginal product of rural workers. The closeness of the relationship is open to question, particularly when one allows for urban unemployment and the desire of employers to reduce the loss of skill through labour turnover.[7] But it is generally accepted that some such relationship exists and that actual urban wage rates should be brought into line with shadow wages.

Criterion (i) would prefer to see rises in the standards of living of the lowest-paid urban workers dependent, not on collective bargaining, but on improvements in rural incomes. As Turner has noted, this would require a change in the structural role of the minimum wage, away from acting as the determinant of many other wages, towards one of serving as a 'safety net', as the wage level at the first probationary entry into wage employment.

Since the implementation of criterion (i) would, in practice, cause a drop in the wages of the lowest-paid workers, without (initially, at least) any corresponding drop in other urban wages, it is often felt that criterion (i) must be rejected, since it aggravates the already unequal distribution of income within the urban sector. Accordingly, Ghai has proposed a compromise solution of relating the changes in urban incomes to changes in rural earnings,[8] although the merits of any policy which maintains rural/urban differentials unaltered are dubious.

A more substantial criticism of criterion (i) is that offered by Guy Routh, who believes that peasant families—or the male members of such families—positively prefer the rural way of life to the offer of an urban job with the same real income. 'The "under-employment" from which well-meaning economists are trying to rid them is one of the main advantages of their way of life . . . It would be inappropriate to make agricultural development a *condition* for the rise of living standards of employees.'[9] Routh's comments certainly have a measure of truth, but the weight of evidence of migration studies in Africa suggests that large numbers of peasant farmers do migrate in response to rural/urban earnings differentials. Thus rural underemployment may be less voluntary than Routh presumes.

It is another criticism of criterion (i) (that it may be largely irrelevant in the context of profit-maximising behaviour by employers) which enjoys the most widespread academic support. In a sense, the labour-turnover models, like that of Stiglitz mentioned above, would reinforce this criticism. For the labour-turnover models demonstrate that, where employers make sizable investments in training their work force and have, consequently, a strong interest in keeping labour turnover low, the wages that employers are willing to pay may lie substantially above the alternative real incomes of workers in agriculture. While wage levels in such models would be related to rural incomes, they would be so far above rural incomes as to make minimum wage fixing according to criterion (i) irrelevant for wage determination in many sectors.

However, the most popular argument put forward to support the view that minimum wages in developing countries will, in practice, bear little relation to rural incomes is the 'efficiency wage' approach which asserts that there is a range of incomes over which labour efficiency rises faster than the cost of labour to the employer. It is often alleged that, at very low wage levels, wage increases yield such dramatic improvements in the nutritional standards and physical fitness of workers and give rise to such dramatic improvements in employers' management of workers that the labour costs per unit output may actually fall, even in the absence of increased mechanisation.[10] Thus Reginald Green has stated that

> The bulk of the evidence – contrary to the 'Lazy African', 'backward bending supply curve' mythology – is that African urban wages are too low. Higher wages would in many cases lead to more than offsetting increases in productivity both because workers would stay on one job longer, acquire more skills, attain better nutritional and health standards and because management would provide better training supervision and work allocation to economise on the use of new 'higher cost' employees.[11]

From Tanzania, there is some evidence to support Green. In 1962, the Tanzanian Government accepted the recommendations of the Chesworth Report, which raised minimum wages substantially, with increases of 100 per cent in the case of some labourers on sisal plantations. Subsequently employment on the sisal estates, Tanzania's main employers of wage labour, fell sharply. Reviewing the impact of his award, Chesworth[12] has shown that the net effect of the higher wages and lower employment was to leave the labour costs per unit of sisal output unaltered, without any corresponding increase in the capital intensity of production.

Despite this evidence which might be interpreted as confirming Green's statement, one is left pondering the question why, if it was in their own best interests to do so, the employers in Tanzania had not chosen to raise wages before being obliged to do so by government action. In the Tanzanian case, it would seem to be correct to attribute the 1962 minimum wage award, not to any awareness that it would in the long run be justified by higher workers' efficiency, but to the conscious decision of the Tanzanian government 'that it was better to start from a smaller employed labour-force on adequate minimum wages than from a large exploited one'.[13]

Since, in 1962, the wages of sisal workers were probably no lower than the alternative incomes available in agriculture, it is clear that the Tanzanian government, in doubling minimum wages, was not using criterion (i) to determine minimum wages. From the use of the adjective 'adequate' the Tanzanians seem to have preferred 'the needs of the workers' criterion for minimum wage fixing; but this is fraught with at least as many difficulties as criterion (i).

(ii) 'The Needs of Workers'. The most common interpretation of the wage level corresponding to 'the needs of workers' is the Poverty Datum Line wage – the minimum cost of providing a certain minimum standard of health and decency to a household. Given the vagueness of the Poverty Datum Line concept, it is scarcely surprising that there is no unambiguous measure of it. But a more serious problem is that, where the Poverty Datum Line has been acceptably estimated, in most developing countries it appears to recommend granting excessive increases in minimum wages. For example, in 1957/8 Bettinson estimated that the Poverty Datum Line wage for a couple in Lusaka with two children was a monthly £12 6s 10½d which compared with the *average* cash wage of African males of only £7 2s 5d.[14] Of all the African households surveyed with two adults and two children 78 per cent had incomes below the Poverty Datum Line.

The ILO, with its theme of a 'basic needs' employment and incomes strategy, sponsored during the mid-1970s and reflected in the Zambia Employment Mission report of 1976, provides one possible means of bringing criteria (i) and (ii) closer together. First, the ILO attempts to answer some of the criticisms that have been made of Poverty Datum Line measures by incorporating within the concept of 'basic needs' the provision of social services, such as education, decent housing, transport facilities, water supplies, sanitation and health services, that are not included in the estimation of Poverty Datum Line wages. Second, the ILO policy recognises that progress towards bringing minimum wages into line with workers' needs will have to be tied to progress in bringing non-wage incomes in the rural sector up to the same levels. Thus the ILO's 'basic needs' approach to incomes policy is intended to serve more as a guideline towards the long-run improvement of minimum income levels throughout an economy than as a means of establishing a new rule for minimum wage determination that raised urban wages even further above rural incomes than they already are.

In Zambia, it is true that the 1974/5 Mwanakatwe Salaries Commission used Poverty Datum Line estimates to justify its very generous pay awards to the lowest-paid government employees. But much more typical, in Zambia and elsewhere, was the behaviour of the 1963/4 Hadow Salaries Commission, which never considered criterion (i) as a basis of its wage awards, and rejected criterion (ii) once it realised how expensive it would be to implement. Its eventual recommendations were based instead on 'the criteria of financial and economic justification'.[15]

(iii) 'Capacity to Pay'.

Unfortunately, 'the criteria of financial and economic justification' or of 'the capacity to pay' are more indeterminate than either criterion (i) or (ii). Their most obvious interpretation is that the more profitable is a firm, or the lower is its labour intensity, the greater is its 'capacity to pay'. As the discussion in Chapters 5 and 6 reveals, the structure of wages in Zambia corresponds closely to one consistent with the 'capacity to pay' approach. Sectors pay higher wages as their labour intensity decreases. Yet, while the capacity to pay successfully describes how sectors determine their wages relative to one another, it does not appear to offer much assistance when it comes to deciding how the government ought to use its abilities to influence minimum wage rates. The labour intensity of production will be a useful indication of the bargaining power of workers vis-à-vis their employers, but it would be a strange view of the government's social responsibilities to argue that the government ought to use its influence in wage setting to relate wages more closely to employers' 'capacity to pay'. Employers with a high 'capacity to pay' will also tend to have a high 'capacity to pay tax'. Accordingly, the government's priorities in these circumstances ought to be to raise more tax revenue, to be used for the general good, rather than to increase the wages of an already somewhat privileged few.

The Control of Wages and Salaries Above the Minimum

The theoretical issues behind the government's role in the control of wages and salaries above the minimum are mostly similar to those raised in the discussion of minimum wages. In part this is because, as we noted above, minimum wage awards determine directly up to one-half of all urban wages; but the main reason is that the principles enunciated in the discussion of minimum wages apply equally to wages above the minimum. Thus wages above the minimum should, in the opinion of many theorists, be determined in the light of transfer earnings available elsewhere, the desire to achieve the best trade-off between wage costs, training expenditures and labour turnover, and the need to retain an incentive structure that will encourage suitable people to increase their skills.

At present, wage scales in developing economies have little in common with one based on the theoretical principles just listed. The retention and extension of pay scales developed during colonial times have tended to introduce biases in favour of white-collar staff, particularly where wages in such jobs have been tied to expatriates' earnings or the (increasing) level of workers' educational qualifications.[16] The state's influence in wage fixing often aggravates the situation. Green's comments apply to many countries:

> Regardless of the wisdom of past wage increases, there is reason to wonder whether the present machinery for determining wages in East Africa is not heavily biased in favour of wage increases, whether nationally desirable or not. Ministries of Labour have tended . . . to hold the standard European position that labour (including organised urban labour) is an economically underprivileged and weak group . . . The view of employed labour as underprivileged and weak is highly inaccurate. Relative to the vast majority of the population, wage employees . . . comprise a privileged group.[17]

Faced with this marked divergence between theory and practice, it is somewhat surprising to read the policy recommendations of H.A. Turner, the academic with the greatest single influence on wage policy in the developing world. Turner, who, one will recall, was very much in favour of bringing minimum wage rates into line with earnings available in alternative agricultural employment, has a very different view regarding wages above the minimum. He recommends, both in his Cambridge Occasional Paper and in his reports on incomes policy in countries such as Zambia and Tanzania, relating wage increases directly to improvements in labour productivity, and proposes the introduction of payment-by-results schemes wherever practicable.

At a practical level, the measurement of labour productivity is often extremely difficult, especially when it comes to taking account of the effects of increased mechanisation.[18] But, theoretically, there can be seen to be something of an inconsistency between proposing a reduction in minimum wages, in order to bring them into line with rural earnings, and, at the same time, advocating a productivity-related scale of increases for all wages above the minimum. While minimum wages will drop initially, and subsequently move parallel to rural incomes, wages above the minimum will tend to move upwards alongside labour productivity. Unless productivity in agriculture rises faster than urban labour productivity, the gap between the mass of rural and urban incomes will remain unchanged, or will even widen. Only workers on minimum wages will have been asked to make a sacrifice in their real incomes in order to make income distribution more equitable.

If the principle behind the minimum wage recommendations is to be applied equally to other wages, and all urban workers' wages are related to their transfer earnings in alternative employment, it follows that the initial thrust of incomes policy will have to be directed towards the reduction of virtually all real urban wages and salaries, both at the minimum and above it.

Incomes Policies in Eastern Africa

The Background

Our discussion of the theoretical bases of incomes policies has focused strongly on the egalitarian, income distributional aspects of such policies. In terms of their effects upon the bulk of the labour force, the main conclusion to be drawn from the theory presented above is that urban wage and agricultural pricing and production policies should be designed much more carefully so as to reduce the disparities between rural and urban incomes while retaining adequate incentives for skills and reduced labour turnover.

Against this background, it is somewhat surprising to discover that the incomes policies that have been proposed in Eastern Africa have grown out of pressure to maintain real urban incomes in the face of inflation and reduced wage employment rather than as a response to egalitarian income distributional policies. In Zambia, for example, the evidence is that the invitation to Professor Turner to visit Zambia and prepare an incomes policy in 1969 was occasioned mainly by the concern in official circles at the 1968 employment and cost of living statistics, which showed that unprecedented inflation had occurred alongside declining employment growth.

In Kenya, the five years 1960-5 saw a doubling of urban African wages, as against only a 35 per cent increase in peasant household incomes. The urban cost of living rose 14 per cent over this period, while total wage employment fell by 10 per cent. Faced with this situation, the government introduced the 1964 Tripartite Agreement, between government, unions and employers, under which employers undertook to increase employment by at least 10 per cent in return for a pledge of no wage demands or strikes for one year.

After the 1964 Tripartite Agreement, wage employment stopped falling, and then started to rise slowly, averaging 2 per cent growth annually over the next 5 years. This growth rate was still inadequate, and so a second tripartite agreement, very like the first, was signed in 1970, containing an undertaking by the government to implement a 'Wages and Incomes Policy' within a year. In 1970, the government also appointed a National Assembly select committee to examine ways of alleviating unemployment. But the promised 'wages and incomes policy' never materialised. Instead, the next initiative came from outside Kenya, from the International Labour Office, which secured the approval of the Kenyan government for the choice of Kenya as the site of the pilot African study in the World Employment Programme.

The ILO document[19] represents the only detailed proposals on incomes policy that have been formulated for Kenya. Accordingly, in the comparative study of incomes policy in Eastern Africa which follows, we shall contrast the Kenyan ILO report with the two ILO-sponsored Turner reports prepared for Zambia and Tanzania.

Tanzania's wage employment problems, like Kenya's, came earlier than Zambia's, and were more serious than those faced in either of the other countries. Having achieved selfgovernment in 1960 with a wage labour force of 417,000, wage employment had fallen to 334,000 by 1966, the date of Turner's arrival in the country. Much of the fall in wage employment was attributable to the 1962 minimum wage awards, mentioned above, but the scale of the fall and its long continuation were greater than the government had expected. Furthermore, the redistribution of national income that had accompanied the fall in wage employment had run counter to the government's intentions. Between 1960 and 1966 the real national income per head had risen at 1 per cent per annum, but while urban workers had seen their average real incomes more than double over this period, and the share of profits in national income had managed to rise slightly, the share of national income going to smallholders and subsistence farmers had fallen from an average of 53 per cent in 1960-2 to a value of 48 per cent in 1965. The search for an incomes policy in 1966 reflected the desire to reverse this trend.

Preparations for Incomes Policy

Although Turner's two reports and the World Employment Programme report were commissioned by the respective governments from the International Labour Office, the two Turner reports were requested by governments which had already made the decision to implement some kind of incomes policy, whereas the Kenyan report was prepared for a government without a similar commitment to incomes policies. Thus, in the Kenyan case, apart from the two tripartite agreements, there was little attempt to prepare the ground for any measures that might have been proposed by the ILO mission.

In Zambia, the first signs of concern at the rate of wage increases and of price inflation appeared with the government's intervention to prevent local authority workers from receiving their full 1967 wage award. The government over the next two years acquired control of the dominant private sector mining and industrial firms operating in the country. Restrictions on the trade union movement were tightened, and for the five months before the presentation of the Turner Report all wages were frozen. The report itself was made public, and dominated the discussions, at the important Second National Convention, which was intended to produce guidelines for the Second National Development Plan.

In Tanzania, the groundwork for an incomes policy had been prepared even more thoroughly.

> In 1965 the Cabinet had instructed the Ministry of Economic Affairs and Development Planning ('Devplan') to prepare a draft National Wages Policy to accord with the Development Plan . . . A draft paper was prepared by Devplan in consultation with the Ministry of Labour, the Treasury and the Central Establishments Division of the President's Office, but NUTA (National Union of Tanganyika Workers) made a

number of objections to the draft which some attempts were made to meet. The Cabinet, however, would not approve the draft paper as amended, feeling that it paid insufficient attention either to the needs of national investment or to the need to consider farmers' incomes in national policy, and asked Devplan to prepare a new paper (a request which led to Professor Turner's mission to Tanzania).[20]

The 1966 Arusha Declaration, presented during the preparation of Turner's report, served to complete the process of laying the foundations for a subsequent incomes policy, by bringing together, and making explicit, the political objectives against which the alternative proposals on incomes policy could be judged.

The Politics of Incomes Policy Formulation

A comparison of incomes policy formulation in Zambia, Tanzania and Kenya supports the belief that a government only gains from foreign 'expert' advice in proportion to its own willingness to provide direction for the 'expert's' investigations. Equally, the Kenyan example illustrates that, with the best will in the world, and the sweetest tongued academics, an 'expert' mission cannot expect to change the development strategy of an unwilling government.

In the Tanzanian case, the host government already had definite ideas about the general form of the incomes policy that it wanted when it invited Professor Turner's mission. Thus government leaders were able to influence significantly the form of his inquiries, shifting the emphasis towards a closer consideration of policy on rural incomes and investment, when they felt these areas were being ignored. And when Turner's report appeared, the government, having been so closely involved in the progress of the mission, responded with carefully considered reactions and proposals of its own. Consequently, the Tanzanian Turner Report and the Tanzanian government's reply to it may be viewed as the final statements in a long, closely argued debate about policy proposals.

The fate of the ILO World Employment Programme mission to Kenya demonstrates the other side of the picture, with a high-powered academic mission working hard to produce proposals which proved to be unacceptable to a government which was always unsympathetic to the main objectives of the mission. The ILO mission did, of course, make every effort to involve agencies of the Kenyan government in its deliberations, but this could never be a substitute for a sincere commitment by policy makers to the income redistribution desired by the academics—with the result that, for all its detailed analysis of the economic and institutional constraints facing Kenya in its future development, the mission's final report remained, as it had started, a largely academic exercise.

The Zambian example illustrates what is likely to happen in the intermediate cases, where the government has a general commitment to the idea of an incomes policy but lacks clear specific objectives. In 1969, the Zambian Government stood at a crossroads in its development strategy. Despite its encouragement of the incipient locally owned capitalist sector, it looked possible that the government would build a socialist state from the basis of the control it had acquired in 1968 and 1969 in the main productive sectors of the economy. Eventually it became evident, with the watering down of the provisions of the Leadership Code and the failure of the 1970 attempt to take over the banking sector, that the government was not attempting a socialist transformation of the economic structure of the country. But in 1969 few people were certain about the future pattern of the country's development.

The political situation in Zambia in 1969 was complicated by the severe tensions that were building up within UNIP, and which culminated in the defection two years later of the Vice-President, Simon Kapwepwe, and his followers who formed the short-lived United Progressive Party. In 1969, therefore, the ILO mission was trying to prepare an incomes report for a government which was divided within itself, and which, although concerned about the problems of inflation and lack of employment creation, had not gone far in formulating its overall policy on income distribution. Consequently the amount of fruitful interaction between the mission and the government, and the use made of the mission's recommendations, were much more limited than in the Tanzanian case.

Incomes Policy Proposals

Of the three cases we are comparing, the most radical proposals on incomes policy, and the closest to the theoretical ideals discussed earlier in this chapter, were those of the ILO mission to Kenya. The World Employment Programme mission was interested in incomes policy, not as an end in itself, but as one of many means of redistributing incomes and income-earning opportunities in favour of the poorest households.

In terms of its proposals for the control of wages, profits and prices, the ILO report was similar to recommendations put forward by Turner in his Cambridge Occasional Paper. It proposed limiting the annual increase in the real wages of workers earning up to £200 per annum to 3 per cent, and progressively to reduce the rate of increase up the wage scale until the £700 level, above which workers would receive no real increase at all for five years. The mission favoured reducing the starting scales in jobs requiring higher qualifications, so that, for a probationary period, new workers in such jobs would receive only 75 per cent of the basic salary. The mission suggested, in addition, that all requests for price increases should be reviewed by a special Price Control Advisory Committee, but that tariffs should be the main instrument used to control the rate of profit in Kenyan industry.

The recommendations on other matters were more original. Central to them was the concept of 'minimum household targets' to be attained by all rural and urban households, and to cover such aspects as incomes, water supplies, nutritional levels and educational opportunity. These led naturally to the advocacy of reforms in the educational system, in the structure of land tenure, in the choice of technique and in the official policy on selfemployment and employment in the informal sector. It is ironic that in this way, the mission, advocating the radical reformist approach to development in preference to a Marxist revolutionary one, found its proposals in conflict with, and ultimately thwarted by, the very class interests whose overthrow lies at the heart of Marxist strategy.[21]

In the Kenyan situation it would have been difficult for the World Employment Programme to have avoided coming into conflict with the vested interests of the ruling elite, but in the Zambian and Tanzanian cases, Turner was able to operate within the framework of government policy, and avoid the pitfall of arousing the insuperable opposition of important interest groups.

With a common author, the Tanzanian and Zambian incomes policy reports were inevitably similar to one another. The diagnosis for both countries was that their problems were caused by wage rises outpacing labour productivity. And Turner's recommendations for overcoming the problem were similar in both cases to those first expounded in his Cambridge Occasional Paper. Wherever possible, he wanted to see workers' earnings linked to a payments-by-results scheme, so that higher productivity would be necessary before workers could secure higher earnings. Prices, he felt, should be permitted to rise only when it could be shown that higher costs could not be absorbed through higher levels of productivity.

On the form of wage scales, Turner's Zambian and Tanzanian proposals were also similar to those originally mentioned in the Cambridge Occasional Paper. A probationary basic scale was advocated, above which would be a series of increments through which a worker could move up or down according to the changes taking place in his efficiency. On price control, the proposals for the two countries were again similar, advocating a system of price control on modern sector products complemented by measures to inform consumers of price changes, thereby serving to bring the pressure of public opinion to bear against excessive price increases.

In all other major respects, however, such as minimum wage determination, the control of excess profits and the treatment of rural incomes, the Zambian and Tanzanian proposals were very different from one another. On minimum wages, the Zambian report had nothing to say about the appropriate method of their determination. Indeed, there are only a couple of passing references to minimum wages in the whole document. The Tanzanian report, however, asserts that

> the only basis for minimum wage policy which seems both objective and practicable in a developing country is a comparison with the living standards of the rural population . . . A minimum wage which gives unskilled and inexperienced workers the same living standard as the small farmer is therefore fair as between the smallholders and the employed workers.[22]

The full force of Turner's minimum wage recommendations, which required a complete reversal of the minimum wage policy established with the 1962 Chesworth award (which had created a disparity between rural earnings and minimum wages), was then somewhat surprisingly weakened by his subsequent statement that

> the main object of wage policy should now be to remove the focus of attention from the minimum wage level to what is much more critical from the point of view both of the general development of the economy and of equitable income distribution – the structure of wages above the minima.[23]

On rural incomes, too, the Zambian report was relatively unenterprising:

> While one may raise the incomes of wage earners by giving them more pay (at least, temporarily, until any resultant rise in the cost of living catches up), or of businessmen by raising prices, the only important and lasting method by which the real incomes of villagers can be raised is by helping and encouraging them to grow and sell more produce, and by making it cheaper and easier for them to get goods or services from the towns.[24]

Accordingly Turner concentrated on suggesting improvements in the rural road network.

In the Tanzanian case, the report's emphasis was on applying the principle of payment-by-results to the rural as well as the urban population. In fact the report was so single minded in the pursuit of *output*-related incentives that the *income* benefits of transfers, such as through subsidies, to rural workers were virtually ignored. Turner felt

> doubtful if a mere subsidy or general tax concession to the farmers (for instance, by way of increasing income tax on employees to reduce tax on agricultural produce) would lead to any real increase in the farmers' output: it might even have the reverse effect. All benefits to farmers should therefore be given in an incentive form . . . For instance benefits should not take the form of subsidies to produce prices (or reductions in produce taxes), but the form of cheap credit for farm investment and subsidies for fertilisers, irrigation works, pesticides, improved strains of seed or stock, and so on, – things which only benefit the farmer if he actually uses them to improve his efficiency . . .
>
> The most useful incentive measure might be a reform of the agricultural tax system. The system under which the farmer's taxes rise the more he produces gives no particular incentive to increased output. A form of agricultural taxation which provides much more incentive to high productivity is a land tax – a flat tax per acre or hectare, so that even the inefficient farmer has to produce enough to pay his taxes, and the efficient farmer earns a great deal more.[25]

The third main difference between the Zambian and Tanzanian Turner reports lay in their treatment of profits. In the Zambian case, there was little more than a statement that

> where there is evidence that agreements by workers to raise efficiency have merely resulted in excessive profits or increased the living standards of employers without otherwise contributing to national development, there should be an investigation to see what has happened and what should be done.[26]

The Tanzanian report, on the other hand, went into considerable detail to devise schemes for collective profit sharing by means of 'workers' shares' and to penalise excessive profits through a special levy on firms with abnormally high profits. It is ironic that the Tanzanian report should have been the one that gave serious consideration to the control of profits when, as Turner himself observed,[27] the 'capitalist consumption' available for reallocation in Tanzania is relatively small, while the report on Zambia, with capitalist consumption both relatively and absolutely much more important than in Tanzania, should virtually have ignored this key aspect of incomes policy.

Official Reactions to Incomes Policy Proposals

After some delay, the Kenyan Government published a cautiously worded official response[28] to the ILO report presented in 1972. In it the government appeared to accept much of the ILO mission's strategy on income redistribution, remarking that 'in most cases proposals in the report reflect, or are consistent with, current Government policies'.[29] But little was done to give effect to any of the report's more substantial recommendations.

In the Zambian case, Professor Turner's report received a largely uncritical response from government leaders. The report had fulfilled its role of identifying a scapegoat – the growing inefficiency of the labour force – to blame for the country's problems of employment creation and inflation, and had made proposals for correcting these failings in the future. The government in its single mindedness was none too concerned about the accuracy of the identification of the scapegoat,[30] and, lacking a clear policy on income distribution as a whole, ignored the report's deficiencies (in comparison with the similar report for Tanzania) in the areas of minimum wage fixing, rural incomes and profit taxation.

The only notable change that the Zambian Government proposed making to Turner's suggestions was in the administration of the incomes policy. Whereas Turner preferred to leave this to one central Wages, Prices and Productivity Board, the Second National Convention wanted to decentralise the functions of administration among a variety of institutions, such as a Prices Board, an Industrial Court and a strengthened Rent Control Board, with a Productivity, Wages and Prices Council to submit guidelines on pay awards to the Industrial Court.

The fates of these institutions have been a poor omen for the success of any incomes policy in Zambia. A Prices Board was established in 1970, and the Industrial Relations Act was passed in 1971. But the Prices Board soon proved to be ineffectual, having been given no meaningful powers to collect evidence on price determination or to give effect to any recommendations. After the chairman submitted her resignation in 1972, the board became defunct. The Industrial Relations Act fared no better. The Industrial Court was not created until April 1974, and its first decision of any significance was made a full 18 months later. As yet, the promised Productivity, Wages and Prices Council to advise the court on wage awards has not been created.

The only policy, of those proposed at the Second National Convention, which still exists in a tangible form five years later is the 5 per cent limit on annual pay rises, proposed as something of a stop-gap measure, while a scheme of productivity-related wage awards was devised. However, the Ministry of Labour and Social Services, responsible for the implementation of the wage policy, has been given no statutory powers to enforce it; and, as we remarked in Chapters 6 and 7, even the government itself, as, for example, in the case of the wage awards to senior civil servants, has shown no respect for the policy guidelines.

The Tanzanian Government prepared the most detailed response to its incomes policy report. It largely accepted Turner's criticisms of past policies, although it defended part of the fall in employment as a logical consequence of its belief that 'after Independence . . . it was better to start from a smaller employed labour force on adequate minimum wages than from a large exploited one'.[31] Despite this, the government was in sympathy with Turner's suggestions on minimum wage policy, which were felt to be 'strictly in accordance with the spirit of the Arusha Declaration'. Accordingly it announced that it would carry out statistical surveys as soon as possible to determine the average smallholder's living standard to provide the basis for the new system.[32]

The government decided to control wages above the minimum by means of a Permanent Labour Tribunal, established in October 1967, which would vet all voluntary pay agreements, while operating within the following guidelines, among others:

(a) Increases in wages and fringe benefits should not exceed 5 percent in any year; the 5 percent to be determined as an average of the total wage bill (including the cost of fringe benefits) for the group of employees to whom the claim relates . . .
(b) The only permitted exception to the 5 percent maximum will be in the case of workers for whom *bona fide* payment by results schemes are introduced, under which the workers concerned agree to increase their personal output and efficiency at least proportionately to the increase in labour costs involved.[33]

Payment by results schemes, however, were to permit increases in earnings only up to the following limits, so as to give preference to lower-paid workers:

Present monthly rate	Permitted earnings increase
Up to Shs. 150/-	20%
Shs. 151/- to Shs. 200/-	15%
Shs. 201/- to Shs. 250/-	10%
Shs. 251/- and above	5%

. . . though schemes will only be approved where a measurable output is involved.[34]

The Tanzanian Government found itself in close agreement with Turner's proposals on price control, and took steps to implement them. But in respect of policy on such crucial matters as investment and rural development, the report was found lacking. The Government Paper published in reply to Turner's report, therefore, took the opportunity to clarify the principles set out in the Arusha Declaration, and to provide a detailed elaboration of the institutional framework that it felt to be necessary for rural development. In addition, it presented a statement of its new policy guidelines on investment, both as regards redressing the balance between urban and rural projects and in relation to the delimitation of those sectors in which private investment would be permitted.

The Tanzanian policy is the only one which is sufficiently explicit, and which has lasted long enough to be able to be judged fairly from the trend in output, employment, wages and prices since the policy was implemented. The data for the period before the bad harvests and world inflation of 1973/4 are summarised in Table 7.1, page 162. On the evidence of this table, the Tanzanian incomes policy has been largely successful. Real wages, having risen steadily until 1967, dropped slightly over the next five years, while wage employment rose by 20 per cent. The real wage bill, therefore, increased by nearly 13 per cent. Real GDP, however, rose by 24.5 per cent, which permitted the economy to enjoy an upsurge in the share of gross capital formation in GDP from the levels of 12 to 15 per cent around which it languished during the early 1960s to near 30 per cent in the early 1970s.

The possibilities for luxury consumption expenditures, or for the accumulation of sizable private business and property holdings have been drastically reduced, and the tax system has been made more sharply progressive, so that inequalities in disposable incomes have been reduced. The *ujamaa* programme has seen a shift of agricultural policy

Table 7.1: Economic Indicators for Tanzania, 1960-72

Year	1960	1961	1962	1963	1964	1965	1966	1967	1968	1969	1970	1971	1972
Total wage employment (000)	417.0	411.5	397.0	340.3	351.3	333.8	336.5	346.8	251.6	367.9	375.6	401.9	414.3
GDP (at factor cost) in Tshs (000 mn) at 1966 constant prices				5.70	6.06	6.18	6.72	6.83	7.17	7.34	7.78	8.08	8.50
Cost of living index of wage earners				100.0	102.5	109.4	114.7	116.6	122.0	124.4	128.4	135.5	143.0
Average wage per worker (shillings/ annum)	1,600	1,820	2,100	2,680	2,760	3,000	3,330	3,600	3,740	3,780	4,000	4,100	4,180
Average wage in constant 1966 prices				2,680	2,690	2,740	2,900	3,090	3,060	3,030	3,110	3,030	2,920

in favour of the poor. But in one respect the Tanzanian Government found it hard to remain within its avowed incomes policy. Minimum wage rates in 1967 were at the levels fixed by the 1962 Chesworth award, 80 shillings per month in non-plantation agriculture, rising to 150 shillings in some urban jobs. Despite its 1967 acceptance of the principle that minimum wages should be related to smallholders' incomes, all minimum wage rates were increased by 20 shillings in 1969, and moved up again to a range of 140 shillings to 270 shillings in 1972. However, minimum wage policy is the only serious failing in what must otherwise be considered to have been a successful implementation of a comprehensive incomes policy.

Notes

1. In the Zambian context, it seems reasonable to suppose that farmers' propensities to save are much higher than those of most maize consumers. Thus a policy of passing higher producer prices directly on to customers is likely to increase the overall level of savings within the country.

2. In 'An Analysis of Employment and Income Distribution in Zambia' (unpublished DPhil thesis, Nuffield College, Oxford, 1974).

3. J. Rawls, *A Theory of Justice* (Harvard University Press, Cambridge, Mass., 1971).

4. E. Berg, 'Major Issues of Wage Policy in Africa' in A.M. Ross (ed.), *Industrial Relations and Economic Development* (Macmillan, London, 1966).

5. ILO, *Minimum Wage Fixing and Economic Development* (ILO, Geneva, 1968), p. 59.

6. Expressed, for example, by H.A. Turner in *Wage Trends, Wage Policies and Collective Bargaining: the Problems for Underdeveloped Countries*, University of Cambridge Department of Applied Economics Occasional Paper No. 6, (1965); P.H. Thormann, 'The Rural-Urban Income Differential and Minimum Wage Fixing Criteria', *International Labour Review*, vol. CII, July-December (1970); and M. Todaro, 'Income expectations, Rural-Urban Migration and Employment in Africa', *International Labour Review*, vol. CIV, July-December (1971).

7. As is done in J.E. Stiglitz, 'Wage Determination and Unemployment in L.D.C.'s', *Quarterly Journal of Economics*, May (1974).

8. D.P. Ghai, 'Incomes Policy in Kenya: Need, Criteria and Machinery', *Eastern Africa Economic Review*, vol. 1.1, June (1968).

9. G. Routh, *Incomes Policy in a Developing Country: A Case Study of the Foreign Expert at Work (Turner in Tanzania)* (Institute for Development Studies, University of Sussex, 1969).

10. For a theoretical exposition of this theory see J.A. Mirrlees, *A Pure Theory of Underdevelopment* (Nuffield College, Oxford, 1973).

11. R.H. Green, 'Wage Levels, Employment, Productivity and Consumption', in J.R. Sheffield (ed.), *Education, Employment and Rural Development* (East African Publishing House, Nairobi, 1967), pp. 215 and 217.

12. D. Chesworth, 'Statutory Minimum Wage Fixing in Tanzania', *International Labour Review*, vol. XCVI, July-December (1967).

13. *Wages, Incomes, Rural Development, Investment and Price Policy* (Tanzania

Government Paper No. 4, 1967), p. 2, para. 8.

14. D.G. Bettinson, 'The Poverty Datum Line in Central Africa', *Rhodes-Livingstone Journal*, no. 27, June (1960), pp. 1-40.

15. *Report of the Commission Appointed to Review the Salaries and Conditions of Service of the Northern Rhodesia Public and Teaching Services, and of the Northern Rhodesia Army and Air Force* (Government Printer, Lusaka, 1964), Ch. III, para. 36.

16. See Turner, *Wage Trends, Wage Policies and Collective Bargaining*, p. 19; and A.R. Jolly, *Employment, Wage Levels and Incentives* (SOAS and IDS, University of Sussex, Joint Reprint Series No. 26), 1968.

17. Green, 'Wage Levels', pp. 223-4.

18. These difficulties are discussed in the context of Turner's Zambian report in J. Fry, 'The Turner Report, A Zambian View', *Eastern Africa Economic Review*, December (1970), pp. 53-82.

19. ILO, *Employment, Incomes and Equality* (ILO, Geneva, 1972).

20. Para. 31 of Tanzania Government Paper No. 3 of 1967 on *Wages, Incomes and Prices Policy* (Government Printer, Dar es Salaam). This report, written by Turner, will be referred to as 'the Tanzanian Turner Report'.

21. For an extremely elegant and powerful critique of the ILO Kenyan report on the grounds of its 'political utopianism' and 'misrepresentation of the modes of production in Kenya', see C. Leys, *Underdevelopment in Kenya* (Heinemann, London, 1975), particularly pp. 258-71.

22. Tanzanian Turner Report, p. 19, para. 46.

23. Tanzanian Turner Report, para. 61.

24. H.A. Turner, *Report to the Government of Zambia on Incomes, Wages and Prices in Zambia: Policy and Machinery*, Ch. XI, para. 97 (Government Printer, Lusaka, 1969). Henceforth referred to as *Zambian Turner Report.*

25. Tanzanian Turner Report, Appendix C.

26. Zambian Turner Report, p. 29, para. 60.

27. Tanzanian Turner Report, pp. 31-2, para. 85.

28. Sessional Paper No. 10 of 1973, *Employment* (Government Printer, Nairobi, 1973).

29. *Employment*, p. (ii).

30. This is discussed in Fry, 'The Turner Report: A Zambian Review'.

31. Para 8 of Tanzania Government Paper No. 4, 1967, *Wages, Incomes, Rural Development, Investment and Price Policy*, which represented the government's reply to the Tanzanian Turner Report.

32. Tanzanian Government Paper No. 4, paras. 19 and 20.

33. Tanzanian Government Paper No. 4, para. 29.

34. Tanzanian Government Paper No. 4, para. 29.

8 PRICES AND INCOMES POLICY—SOME PROPOSALS

There are two main important, if somewhat obvious, conclusions which the brief review of incomes policy in Eastern Africa given in Chapter 7 should bring to our notice. The first, epitomised by the contrast between the Tanzanian and Kenyan cases, is that the success of an incomes policy depends crucially on the degree of the commitment by a government to the objective of reducing income inequality. The second, which a comparison between the Zambian and Tanzanian experiences serves to emphasise, is that incomes policies have to be comprehensive to be effective.

In this chapter, I shall present a number of more specific conclusions about the form of a successful incomes policy and try to relate these to the Zambian situation where possible. I shall not go into the question of whether or not a gradualist or a more revolutionary method of income redistribution is more desirable. Political expediency will temper a government's ability to achieve dramatic, revolutionary changes in the pattern of income distribution; but there is clearly a point at which a government's view of the institutional/structural constraints operating upon its freedom of action becomes so narrow that it is impossible to discuss meaningful redistribution of incomes without, at the same time, proposing revolutionary political changes.

The ILO/World Bank response to the dilemma described in the previous chapter has been to put forward income redistributional strategies which aim only to redistribute the gains from growth. No one's absolute level of real income is actually reduced under their proposals, but the intention is so to increase the lowest incomes earned in the labour force that relative income differentials decrease.[1] However, where rates of investment and per capita growth rates of national income are low, the pace at which differentials are reduced by this strategy is likely to be considered unacceptably slow.

Agricultural Pricing and Production Policy

The considerations mentioned in the section on theory ought to apply more forcefully here than they usually do in policy formulation. The land tax proposed for Tanzania, or the improved feeder road system proposed for Zambia, are peripheral to the main issues of income redistribution. While it is undoubtedly true that redistribution is most desirable when it can be tied to incentives for increased production, substantial welfare gains may nevertheless be achieved from using agricultural pricing policy as a form of negative income tax, to make transfers of income to those most in need.

The practical difficulties that have to be overcome are considerable. Both incentive schemes and the use of prices and subsidies to achieve income transfers are hard to devise so as to ensure that they are administratively simple while not proving to be primarily of benefit to the most prosperous farmers. But it should not be impossible, for example, to create means of associating with a price system within which a large element of income transfer is hidden an income tax schedule applied to larger-scale farmers which claws back the transfer from them.

A more serious criticism of the use of agricultural pricing policy to attain income distributional objectives is that those most deserving of transfers are the least involved in the market economy, and thus are the hardest to reach through policies operating on market variables. To some extent this can be alleviated by differentiated regional pricing policies, favouring those regions more remote from the main markets for agricultural produce or with a higher than usual proportion of low-income farmers. A careful differentiation of pricing policy by crops is also required, so that the labour-intensive crops produced by small-scale farmers (in Zambia, these would include cotton, groundnuts, burley and turkish tobacco, fish, rice and coffee) can be singled out for especially favourable treatment.

In the extreme case of a pure subsistence farmer with no involvement in cash agriculture, market manipulations cannot affect his income, however they are devised. Hence a reorientation of the agricultural extension service towards the least successful agricultural households, supplemented by free social services or direct income transfers will have to be used to raise the standards of living of such people. But pure subsistence farmers are few and far between nowadays, so that there is every reason to believe that a well designed agricultural pricing policy can play an important part in transferring income to the poor. In addition, it is worth remarking that a pricing policy which stimulates the production of labour-intensive commodities by large-scale farmers will also tend to help the poorest farmers by offering them better paid opportunities as agricultural labourers.

Thus there are a variety of agricultural policy measures – regionally differentiated producer prices, a redirection of the agricultural extension effort, subsidies tied to income taxation, and differential crop price intervention for both large and small producers – all of which deserve to be employed actively to improve the national pattern of income distribution.

Price Control and Profit Taxation

These two elements can be discussed together, since they both relate to measures designed to limit the share of profits in national income. The former is administratively unwieldy: so much so that the expense of a price control department can really be justified only for items which account for a significant part of consumer expenditure. There is little point, for example, in controlling the wholesale and retail prices of commodities such as breakfast cereals or tomato ketchup (as the Zambian authorities attempt to do), when a different price has to be fixed for every brand and every size of the commodities, and when the consumption of these goods is negligible.

Price control is of real value only when the range of goods controlled is very limited, consisting of staples like soap, detergents, cooking oil, margarine, tea, sugar, salt, flour and bread, which are produced by domestic monopolies or collusive oligopolies, and which ideally are capable also of having the nationally determined price printed prominently on the wrapping around the commodities. In these few cases, it is politically wise to create price control machinery, and to rely upon price control to reduce the level of monopoly profits. For the majority of goods, however, there are better, less cumbersome ways of trying to restrain both retailers' and manufacturers' margins.

Retailers' margins may be expected to fall when competition is increased in the retail sector. At present, a politically motivated licensing system restricts entry into retailing in most developing countries, maintaining prices and profits at high levels for those fortunate enough to receive licences, but restricting the opportunities for small traders to set themselves up in competition. Indeed, unlicensed petty traders are frequently rounded up and arrested to protect the interests of the privileged few in countries like Zambia. The abandonment of these restrictive licensing regulations, and their replacement by simple hygiene and safety laws applicable to all retail businesses, would be a commendable step.

In the case of manufacturers, margins are protected from foreign competition by means of tariffs. Tariff reductions are therefore the ideal instrument when it is desired to reduce domestic prices and profits. For non-traded goods and services which do not enter into foreign trade, such as most services, construction and electricity, the use of tariffs will have no effect on domestic prices. As with retailing, the best hopes of price control would appear to lie in the encouragement of competition in the appropriate sector. Failing this, either state control or the introduction of a scale of government-approved charges are the most satisfactory alternatives for achieving the same goals.

Besides its administrative complexity, the main problem as regards the use of price control as a means of influencing income distribution is that it proves to be too blunt an instrument for the sensitive role it has to play. By fixing one, or both, of input and output prices the government is having to make a difficult choice about the level of profit that is 'right' for a particular firm. Yet it is inevitable, given the nature of these decisions that they will rarely be very accurate, if only because prices are rounded upwards or downwards for simplicity, and because it takes a while to respond to changes in circumstances. Profit taxation, by concentrating directly upon the variable which incomes policy seeks to control, is much more effective in attaining a desired distribution of income between wages and profits.

The choice of a suitable system of profit taxation is, as the earlier theoretical discussion indicated, a difficult problem. Income distributional objectives have to be balanced against the desire to increase the share of investment in national income. Attitudes towards foreign investment have to be clarified, and the amount of profits allowed to be remitted out of the country has to be determined in the light of estimates about the true transfer earnings of foreign capital and expertise.

It is hard to make any categorical statements about the form of profits tax that will emerge once account is taken of all these considerations. It is quite likely that the most desirable tax system will apply different tax schedules to profits according to the sector in which they are earned, or the region in which the original investment was made, or the labour and skill intensity of production. However, one can confidently assert that any optimal profits tax schedule should apply very high marginal rates of taxation to excess profits (those profits over and above the value of the transfer earnings of the capital invested, where allowance is made for a reasonable risk premium). In addition, it is wise, once the decision has been made to tolerate private investment, to acquire this investment on the most favourable terms. One way of achieving this is by encouraging competition among potential investors, but equally important are measures designed to reduce the high risk premium required by most investors in developing countries. A national investment code, to specify the terms and conditions under which private investment is to be permitted, while accepting certain restrictions on the government's freedom of action, would seem to be one of the most effective means of reducing the risk premium. In return for commitments, for example, on the level of compensation to be paid in the event of a government takeover or participation, or on the range within which exchange control regulations, profits taxation or depreciation allowances may be varied, it may be possible to secure the acceptance by private investors of fairly low rates of return on capital above which excess profits taxation would become effective.

Minimum Wage Determination

The level of minimum wages plays a key role in determining the magnitude of the three main income gaps in a developing economy. It influences the size of the gap between high- and low-income wage workers, the size of the gap between the earnings of employees in large-scale 'modern' enterprises and small-scale 'traditional' enterprises, and the size of the gap between the earnings of unskilled rural dwellers and unskilled urban 'modern' sector workers.

The most popular academic proposals on statutory minimum wage determination (basing wages on earnings in other, i.e. rural, sectors of the economy) we have seen would have the effect of reducing both of the last two gaps, but at the high political price of imposing sizable reductions in their living standards upon the large number of wage earners whose wages are near the statutory minimum. The alternative proposals of relating minimum wages to the 'needs of the workers' or to the employer's 'capacity to pay' are, in practice, much harder to implement, and lack the egalitation welfare justification of the most favoured approach. Yet the 'capacity to pay' cannot be dismissed entirely as a factor to be considered in minimum wage fixing. Even within the present structure of minimum wages, it is evident that differences have developed between sectors, quite independently of government intervention. The *de facto* minimum wages in the copper mining industry and Zambia Railways are well above the highest statutory minimum wage; and the statutory minimum wages in agriculture, retailing and construction all differ considerably between one another, in response to pressures from employers in those sectors.

There is a danger of treating 'the capacity to pay' approach as a tautology – so that one says that one sector has a greater 'capacity to pay' than another because it pays a higher minimum wage – but there are some objective measures, such as high capital/labour ratio, a low share of wages in total production costs, or a high rate of return on capital, which might be felt to indicate a sector's 'capacity to pay' and which correlate closely with its minimum wage level. Furthermore, the correlation is maintained if one considers wages, not only at, or above, legal minima, but also below legal minima. Chapter 4 describes the extent of wage employment in which workers receive less than legal minimum wages in the Zambian urban and rural traditional sectors, where employers have low 'capacities to pay' by virtue of low capital/labour ratios and a high share of labour costs in total production costs.

The weight of the evidence of Zambian wage data points clearly to the 'capacity to pay' affecting actual minimum wage levels, regardless of the government's intervention via statutory minimum wage policy. Some employers will find it attractive to reduce labour turnover by offering minimum wages above the legal minima; others will choose to flout minimum wage orders and pay their workers less than the legal minima. While the former group of employers may be welcomed, the main concern of minimum wage policy ought to be how to protect the employees of the latter group. To answer this concern, I would like to put forward three alternative minimum wage policies, ranked in order of decreasing political acceptability, and of increasing egalitarian desirability.

Multilevel Minimum Wage Policy

A first proposal might be to rationalise the present *de facto* minimum wage structure, and at the same time extend to traditional sector workers the protection that a statutory minimum wage affords. In practical terms the main impact of such a policy would be to create a new set of minimum wages to apply to traditional sector workers, while leaving modern sector workers unaffected. It can be claimed that, properly implemented, a multilevel minimum wage structure applied to all workers will make little difference to the wages received by the vast bulk of the labour force. However, for a number of workers in the traditional sector, whose present conditions of employment are extremely unpleasant, but to whose plight present labour policy turns a blind eye, a multilevel minimum wage policy offers a means of securing official intervention to improve conditions.

If one estimates that the extra cost of living in towns (for housing, transport and water supplies), as compared with rural areas, is K10 per month, then the data on traditional and modern sector earnings in Zambia suggest that Table 8.1, page 171, might correspond well to the minima under a multilevel system.

Table 8.1: Suggested Minimum Wages for Rural and Urban Areas under Multilevel System

	Region	
Type of employment	Rural	Urban
'Traditional' firm	K1.00/day	K1.40/day
'Modern' firm	K1.40/day	K1.80/day

'Safety-net' Minimum Wage

Turner proposed in his Tanzanian report and Cambridge Occasional Paper that the role of the statutory minimum wage should be confined to that of a 'safety net'. Wages above the minimum would then be determined entirely by market forces and employers' 'capacities to pay'. With the removal of statutory support for minimum wages higher up the scale, a desirable reduction might well occur in income inequality above the new minimum wage.

Against this must be set the possibility that lower wages would not be reflected in lower prices, so that the share of profits in national income would increase. Without the intervention of taxation, this would correspond to a redistribution of income from the poor to the rich. Consequently it can be seen to be important that a policy which redistributes away from wage earners is accompanied by a reduction in tariffs to reduce manufacturers' profits, or by tax changes to cream off any surplus profits.

The No-Minimum-Wage Policy

The major practical difficulty of the 'safety net' minimum wage is to determine the level of the safety net. Should the net be set at average earnings (with due allowance for extra urban costs of living) in the rural areas? Clearly not, since this would leave all employed urban workers better off than a large proportion of the rural population (i.e. better off than the half or so of the rural population earning less than the average rural income level). Should the net then be set at marginal rural earnings? The answer depends on a comparison of the lifetime income prospects of the marginal individuals in rural or urban employment. If, as seems likely, the lifetime income prospects are better in the urban situation, on account of the prospect of receiving training or of moving into better-paid modern sector employment, then even this low safety net is too high since it still favours the urban worker.

The only safety net which is egalitarian between rural and urban workers is one which is so low as not to be effective. The fairest minimum wage for the entire labour force is no minimum wage at all!

The Control of Wages and Salaries Above The Minimum

Faced with these proposals for a reduction in the artificial support for urban wage levels provided by statutory minimum wages, the control of wages and salaries above the minimum acquires a greater than usual importance. Unfortunately the appropriate criteria for the achievement of such control are difficult to devise since there is no consistent rationale behind the structure of the wage and salary scales in most developing countries. While earnings at the top end of the scale are linked closely to those in developed economies, those at the bottom are related tenuously to incomes in the rural sector. The provision of fringe benefits exaggerates the underlying disparities.

We have just discussed earnings at the bottom of the scale; accordingly in this section we shall concentrate upon the higher income levels. There are many topics that we might consider in this context, one very obvious one being the popular suggestion that wages be related to labour productivity. However, measurement problems apart, this, and many other similar suggestions, are unacceptable since they start from the implicit assumption that the current distribution of income is the best that can be achieved. This can be appreciated by observing that, if labour productivity in all sectors changes equiproportionally, relative income distribution will not alter as long as wages are tied to labour productivity.

Much the most important problem in wage determination today is that of devising an adequate incentive structure while reducing the spread of modern sector incomes. Since the previous section has been arguing that, if wages at the bottom of the scale are altered, they should be altered downwards, it follows that our interest in this section must be in reducing higher wages and salaries. In particular, we shall examine the questions of sectoral differentials, the relationship of earnings to educational qualifications, income taxation, and the relationship between local and foreign salary scales.

Before embarking upon the analysis of methods for the reduction of high wages, it should be emphasised that typically the nature of the short-term problem is somewhat different from that of the long-term problem. In the short run, the effect of the past neglect of educational services has been to create a shortage of suitably qualified local citizens in relation to the needs of the economy. Local skilled workers are thereby strongly placed when it comes to taking advantage of this scarcity in wage bargaining. In the long run there should be no such general shortage of skilled workers. Indeed, the evidence of most developing economies is that there will eventually be a surplus of highly qualified local citizens. However, skilled workers enjoy a privileged position within the political order, so that, if they take advantage of short-run scarcities to boost their incomes, it will be difficult to reduce their incomes later, when the supply/demand balance has altered. The problems of sectoral differentials, and of the relationships between earnings and education, and between local and foreign salaries, are all closely related to the changing pattern of skill scarcities.

To take sectoral differentials first, a major difficulty in current salary determination is that sectors are competing with one another for the skilled staff available. While this is inevitable to some degree, it does not have to be pursued to such lengths that government departments compete with one another, with parastatal corporations, with government-controlled companies and with the private sector over the terms they offer prospective employees. Since the private sector now accounts for only a small, and decreasing, share of employment in most developing economies, far too much of the pressure for salary increases is generated by competition within the government-controlled part of the economy. Thus the major recommendation to be proposed as regards sectoral differentials must be that the entire public sector adopts a non-competitive approach to the recruitment of skilled workers until such time as there is an excess supply of such workers. If effectively implemented, short-run temporary distortions in the labour market need not become embedded in the long-run wage and salary structure.

The relationship of earnings to educational qualifications is another example of the way in which short-run considerations, if unchecked, can introduce permanent distortions into the wage and salary structure. In times of skill shortage, employees and employers are happy to introduce pay scales which reward higher skills with higher earnings, and the most simple, objective evaluation of skills is educational performance. As skill shortages disappear, the skills required for a particular job can be raised. For example, primary school teachers in Zambia have seen the minimum educational qualification required of them rise over a short period from primary school education to two years and then to three years of secondary education. Soon they will be required to have completed the full five years of secondary education. Yet there is no reason why the easing of skill shortages should be accompanied by a steady increase in average earnings, on account of relating earnings to educational attainments. One can state the case even more strongly. While skill incentives are needed when skills are in short supply, they may be positively harmful and distortionary when the skills are readily available. It is common to find that long after a shortage of suitably qualified candidates for civil service clerical posts has vanished, these posts continue to offer higher salaries than do black-collar jobs with the same educational requirements, and with a shortage of applicants. For this the blame must rest on the tying of civil service clerical pay scales to educational qualifications, which, given the relative attraction of clerical earnings, causes an undesirable emphasis in schools on subjects appropriate for white-collar employment, at the expense of more urgently needed technical training. Taking all these factors into consideration, it is evident that every effort ought to be made to avoid tying salaries to educational qualifications.

Income taxation is another topic relevant to our present discussion, since it provides one of the most direct, and most easily accepted, methods of reducing disparities in disposable incomes. It is particularly attractive as an instrument in many developing countries, since the income tax schedules were devised, together with fringe benefits, to be generous so as to appeal to expatriate workers and potential settlers. Where, as in Zambia, a large export-orientated sector supplied the major share of government revenue, the incentive for tough income taxation was reduced even further.

Neither of these considerations ought to be relevant to an independent government concerned to reduce income inequality and increase government revenue. Similar objections can be raised against the anachronistic form of those fringe benefits which, like housing subsidies or furniture allowances, were originally introduced only because it would have been hard to have expected short-service expatriates to have provided facilities such as housing for themselves.

Two particular changes in the tax system are long overdue. The most obvious is a reduction in the level of tax exemption – subject to pressing constraints on the work load and administrative costs of the income tax system – and, more important still, increasing marginal rates of income taxation. The other change to be encouraged is the elimination of differential income tax allowances related to marital status, or to family size, and based on outmoded notions of the role of the married woman. The benefit from such allowances, far from helping those who might be felt to need them most, actually assists high-income earners most, since one has to earn enough to be liable to pay income tax before one can benefit from income tax allowances. Furthermore, in a society with extended family obligations, as in Zambia, it is difficult to argue that the financial burden of people with few allowances for tax purposes is very different from that of a married man with several children, entitled to substantial income tax allowances.

To complete this section, we shall analyse the relationship between local and foreign salary scales. The fact that the relationship is so close in skilled occupations is yet further testimony to the bargaining power of local workers in the context of a short-run skill shortage. Unfortunately, as we have argued above, once these close relationships have been allowed to establish themselves, it becomes hard to break them when the local labour supply position eases.

The strongest argument against permitting local salary scales to move too close to foreign scales is the now familiar one that, by letting them come together, income disparities are widened within the local labour force, and the pressures from lower-paid wage earners for their incomes also to rise in line with foreign workers become harder to resist. There are, in addition, two further reasons, less commonly acknowledged, for believing that local pay scales deserve to be considerably out of line with foreign earnings in similar jobs. The first is that, in the international market for skills, most developing countries will never be able to compete in terms of intangibles, such as social facilities, research opportunities or status, with some developed nations. Consequently, even if a reduction in the rate of emigration of skilled workers is one of the main concerns of policy makers, the use of tangible benefits to staunch the flow may prove to be of little effect when the intangible benefits are so much greater abroad. In practical terms, this would imply that there is little point in competing too actively with foreign pay scales, if other aspects of conditions of employment are important determinants of job satisfaction.

The other reason for keeping local salary scales separated from those of the 'world market' is that it is often true to say that Zambians or expatriates in senior posts in Zambia would have to be content with more lowly positions if they offered themselves for employment elsewhere. Generally speaking, this will be truer of administrative, managerial staff than of professional workers, but it applies to some extent to almost every category of worker. Thus, to say, for example, that because Senior Lecturers in Britain earn the equivalent of K8,000 per annum, Senior Lecturers at the University of Zambia deserve also to receive K8,000 is seriously misleading. The correct comparison might well be with a more junior British Lecturer earning only K4,000.

There are other suggestions that one might make for eliminating those aspects of pay determination which tend to preserve and exaggerate existing wage/salary differentials. However, we have mentioned the main ones in which the direction of desirable policy changes is clear. The real difficulty is in deciding how far political constraints permit decision makers to move towards the ideal. Fortunately, with a little ingenuity, one can move far without arousing undue hostility. For example, one is unlikely to provoke much resentment if, as a first step, one permits existing employees to convert to a new pay scale at their current earnings, while creating a new scale for new employees, in which earnings are not tied to educational qualifications. Similarly, a Minister of Finance need not be dismayed at the prospect of abolishing married persons' and child income tax allowances if he can do so in a manner which so raises the earned income allowance that the average tax payer is unaffected by the change. The bitter medicine of higher real tax payments can be left to the workings of inflation, reinforced by a gradual increase in marginal tax rates at future Budgets.

Sectoral and foreign/local differentials present even less of a problem, since the Zambian Government is already committed to, and to some extent enforces, policies designed to prevent these from forcing up local salaries. What is required is better enforcement.

Conclusions

The previous section has ended on an optimistic note, but, as has often been stressed in this chapter, much depends upon the will of government policy makers to implement a truly comprehensive incomes policy, covering wages, salaries, profits, prices and rural incomes. The comparative study of incomes policy in Zambia, Tanzania and Kenya has demonstrated only too clearly that the success of an incomes policy is closely correlated to the degree of support of the ruling party for an egalitarian redistribution of income, and to the comprehensiveness of the policy proposals. The lack of defined goals and a limited scope both condemn an incomes policy to virtual failure. Yet the conditions that have to be satisfied if these difficulties are to be avoided are severe. A regime needs a strong centralised planning framework to formulate and implement its policy proposals, and, of course, an appropriate ideological basis is required. Taken together, these add up to the conditions for a fairly strongly socialist structure. Attempts, like that by the ILO in Kenya, to graft an incomes policy on to an unsuitable institutional infrastructure are certain to fail. Given the eventual political development of the Zambian regime, the policy based upon Turner's proposals for Zambia was ultimately doomed too. Only the Tanzanian situation was ever close to satisfying the preconditions for an incomes policy mentioned above, and significantly, on the evidence of Chapter 7, only the Tanzanian policy can claim to have come near to having succeeded.

Note

1. This strategy is described in detail in H. Chenery *et al.*, *Redistribution with Growth* (Oxford University Press, Oxford, 1974).

INDEX

For Product Safety Concerns and Information please contact our EU representative GPSR@taylorandfrancis.com Taylor & Francis Verlag GmbH, Kaufingerstraße 24, 80331 München, Germany